Supporting language and literacy development in the early years

Second edition

Supporting early learning

Series editors: Vicky Hurst and Jenefer Joseph

The focus of this series is on improving the effectiveness of early education. Policy developments come and go, and difficult decisions are often forced on those with responsibility for young children's well-being. This series aims to help with these decisions by showing how developmental approaches to early education provide a sound and positive basis for learning.

Each book recognizes that children from birth to 6 years old have particular developmental needs. This applies just as much to the acquisition of subject knowledge, skills and understanding as to other educational goals such as social skills, attitudes and dispositions. The importance of providing a learning environment that is carefully planned to stimulate children's own active learning is also stressed.

Throughout the series, readers are encouraged to reflect on the education being offered to young children, through revisiting developmental principles and using them to analyse their observations of children. In this way, readers can evaluate ideas about the most effective ways of educating young children and develop strategies for approaching their practice in ways that offer every child a more appropriate education.

Published and forthcoming titles:

Elizabeth Brooker: *Supporting Transitions in the Early Years*
Jonathan Doherty and Richard Bailey: *Supporting Physical Development and Physical Education in the Early Years*
Bernadette Duffy: *Supporting Children and Imagination in the Early Years 2nd edition*
Lesley Hendy and Lucy Toon: *Supporting Drama and Role Play in the Early Years*
Vicky Hurst and Jenefer Joseph: *Supporting Early Learning – The Way Forward*
Caroline Jones: *Supporting Inclusion in the Early Years*
Linda Pound and Chris Harrison: *Supporting Music in the Early Years*
Linda Pound: *Supporting Mathematical Development in the Early Years 2nd edition*
Iram Siraj-Blatchford and Priscilla Clarke: *Supporting Identity, Diversity and Language in the Early Years*
John Siraj-Blatchford and Iain MacLeod-Brudenell: *Supporting Science, Design and Technology in the Early Years*
John Siraj-Blatchford and David Whitebread: *Supporting Information and Communications Technology Education in the Early Years*
Marian Whitehead: *Supporting Language and Literacy Development in the Early Years*

Supporting language and literacy development in the early years

Second edition

Marian Whitehead

McGraw Hill

Open University Press
Maidenhead

Open University Press
McGraw-Hill Education
McGraw-Hill House
Shoppenhangers Road
Maidenhead
Berkshire
England
SL6 2QL
email: enquiries@openup.co.uk
world wide web: www.openup.co.uk

and Two Penn Plaza, New York, NY 10121-2289, USA

First published 2009

A catalogue record of this book is available from the British Library

ISBN-10: 0335234275
ISBN-13: 9780335234271

Library of Congress Cataloging-in-Publication Data
CIP data applied for

Typeset by Aptara Inc., New Delhi, India
Printed in the UK by Bell and Bain Ltd, Glasgow

Mixed Sources
Product group from well-managed
forests and other controlled sources
www.fsc.org Cert no. TT-COC-002769
© 1996 Forest Stewardship Council
FSC

The *McGraw-Hill* Companies

For my grandchildren Natalie, Daniel, Dylan and Mattias,
and in memory of Vicky Hurst

Contents

Series editors' preface

This book is one of a series that will be of interest to all those who are concerned with the care and education of children from birth to 6 years old – childminders, teachers and other professionals in schools, those who work in playgroups, private and community nurseries and similar institutions; governors, providers and managers. We also speak to parents and carers, whose involvement is probably the most influential of all for children's learning and development.

Our focus is on improving the effectiveness of early education. Policy developments come and go, and difficult decisions are often forced on all those with responsibility for young children's well-being. We aim to help with these decisions by showing how developmental approaches to young children's education not only accord with our fundamental educational principles, but provide a positive and sound basis for learning.

Each book recognizes and demonstrates that children from birth to 6 years old have particular developmental learning needs, and that all those providing care and education for them would be wise to approach their work developmentally. This applies just as much to the acquisition of subject knowledge, skills and understanding, as to other educational goals such as social skills, attitudes and dispositions. In this series there are several books with a subject-based focus, and the main aim is to show how that subject can be introduced to young children within the framework of an integrated and developmentally appropriate curriculum, without losing its integrity as an area of knowledge in its own right. We also stress the importance of providing a learning environment that is carefully planned for children's own active learning. The present book shows how listening, talking, reading and writing start from the moment a child is born. The author traces this development in young children, and gives us a great deal of help in learning how to promote and support these fundamental abilities, so that our children not only become good communicators, but develop into lifelong and passionate devotees of all forms of literature.

Access for all children is fundamental to the provision of educational opportunity. We are concerned to emphasize anti-discriminatory approaches throughout, as well as the importance of recognizing that meeting special educational needs must be an integral purpose of curriculum development and planning. We see the role of play in learning as a central one, and one which also relates to all-round emotional, social and physical development. Play, along with other forms of active learning, is normally a natural point of access to the curriculum for all children at their particular stage and level of understanding. It is therefore an essential force in making for equal opportunities in learning, intrinsic as it is to all areas of development. We believe that these two aspects, play and equal opportunities, are so important that we not only highlight them in each book in this series, but also include separate books on them as well.

Throughout this series, we encourage readers to reflect on the education being offered to young children, through revisiting the developmental principles that most practitioners hold, and using them to analyse their observations of the children. In this way, readers can evaluate ideas about the most effective ways of educating young children, and develop strategies for approaching their practice in ways that exemplify their fundamental educational beliefs, and offer every child a more appropriate education.

The authors of each book in the series subscribe to the following set of principles for a developmental curriculum.

Principles for a developmental curriculum

- Each child is an individual and should be respected and treated as such.
- The early years are a period of development in their own right, and education of young children should be seen as a specialism with its own valid criteria of appropriate practice.
- The role of the educator of young children is to engage actively with what most concerns the child, and to support learning through these preoccupations.
- The educator has a responsibility to foster positive attitudes in children to both self and others, and to counter negative messages that children may have received.

- Each child's cultural and linguistic endowment is seen as the fundamental medium of learning.
- An anti-discriminatory approach is the basis of all respect-worthy education, and is essential as a criterion for a developmentally appropriate curriculum (DAC).
- All children should be offered equal opportunities to progress and develop, and should have equal access to good-quality provision. The concepts of multiculturalism and anti-racism are intrinsic to this whole educational approach.
- Partnership with parents should be given priority as the most effective means of ensuring coherence and continuity in children's experiences, and in the curriculum offered to them.
- A democratic perspective permeates education of good quality and is the basis of transactions between people.

Vicky Hurst and Jenefer Joseph

Acknowledgements

I wish to thank the children, parents and staff of Hampden Way Nursery School, London, Earlham Early Years Centre, Norwich, St John's RC Infant School, Norwich, and Rosebridge Steiner Kindergarten, Cambridge, for generously allowing me to use their photos, documents and examples of children's work in this book, especially in Chapters 5 and 6, which would not have been possible without them. A special thank you must go to Earlham Early Years Centre for the cover photo.

My thanks must be expressed again to Vicky Hurst and Jenefer Joseph, the series editors, for all their affection, wisdom and support. Vicky died during the writing of the first edition of this book and her loss was heartbreaking, but Jenefer has always remained strong and encouraging.

Warm thanks must also go to Jodi Gurney, Headteacher of Hampden Way Nursery School, Janni Nicol, Early Childhood Representative, Steiner Waldorf Schools Fellowship UK, Felicity Thomas, Headteacher, and Steph Harding, pedagogical leader, Earlham Early Years Centre and Mary Fisher and Shelagh Swallow of St John's RC Infant School, for all their expertise, commitment, generosity and guidance. Warm thanks again to Sally Jenkinson and Allyson Pascoe for the contributions they have made to both editions of this book.

I also wish to thank for their help and interest the staff, children and parents of Christchurch Gardens Steiner Kindergarten, Reading (Figure 5.9), The Lindens Waldorf Kindergarten, Stroud, Sunlands Steiner

Kindergarten, Stroud and Wynstones Steiner School (kindergarten), Gloucester.

My loving thanks, as always, to my family who supply so much of the inspiration and examples of language in action and then allow me to write them up.

Introduction

In my Introduction to the first edition of this book I pointed out that there was no shortage of sound books about language in the early years and the production of yet another called for a little justification. Since then there have been even more good books about language but it is deeply gratifying to find that my broad developmental approach has been appreciated by the early years community and led to this second edition. In the 10 years that separate the two editions the world of early care and education has turned upside down – yet again – and this has led to a fairly radical rewrite! However, this book does not stand alone – it is one of a series of books advocating a developmental approach to young children's education. If we are to continue to develop this approach successfully we must understand the complex nature of children's development in the early years and have a particular focus on communication and language, because they are such very significant features of this picture. This is a book that presents a developmental view of language and, although that is not so unusual, it goes on to combine in one fairly accessible book perspectives on the role of literature and the emergence of literacy in the early years. Such a wide-ranging approach to language development is becoming far less common as the requirements for emphasizing literacy and phonics begin to dominate educational practices and publications in the UK and other English-speaking cultures.

This book covers the age range 0–6 or 7 years, and picks up on the unparalleled speed and complexity of growth in children's thinking, communicative abilities, language, social and cultural awareness and physical skills in this period. While looking at this broad phase of child development the book quite consciously challenges the unhelpful gulf, created by recent and historical legislation in the UK, between care and education for the under-5s and care and education for the over-5s. This has led to young children's development and language being forced to fit in with such arbitrary arrangements. This book goes to the core of the matter and looks at what appears to be crucial in language development in these early years.

This fresh look at the nature of early language development has led me to reformulate my priorities for language in these early years and focus on:

• babies as powerful thinkers;
• the significance of non-verbal communication;
• the importance of language play;
• the roots of emerging literacy;
• the notion of language and education as shared community endeavours.

There are chapters in the book that address these themes specifically (Chapters 1, 2, 4, 7) but they also permeate the total approach.

The complexity of each of the above priorities means that it is not easy to sort out the implications for parenting and early years pedagogy, or what is often called the study of learning and teaching. In order to be more supportive of parents, carers and educators, I have ended the chapters that look at aspects of language development (Chapters 1, 2, 3, 4) with notes on how to start supporting children's learning and language more effectively. Additionally, at the heart of the book is a chapter written to support and encourage parents and professional practitioners by showing examples of good practice (Chapter 5). This chapter presents a case study of three distinctive approaches to early education, including language, literature and literacy, and although they originate in different traditions (the British nursery school and Steiner Waldorf education) they offer considerable food for thought, not least the idea that if education and care are to be truly democratic and inclusive, they must be allowed to learn from different philosophies of childhood and pedagogy, and even encouraged to celebrate their differences, as well as their common assumptions.

The positive experience of studying and cooperating with these distinctive 'schools of thought' and their children, staff and parents, led me to write a new chapter (Chapter 6) on the variety of national legislative requirements for language and literacy emerging in the UK. These national frameworks can restrict the kinds of language and literacy experiences educators and professional carers are able to offer young children in group settings. They also narrow the understanding of many untrained or inexperienced providers, and confuse or mislead parents and the wider community. In order to counter these negative messages the chapter also contains a case study from an infant school (5–7 years) of children and teachers learning together in the final year of the English Foundation Stage. Early education may often be driven – and distorted – by political expediency and ideology, to the detriment of children and the adults working with them, but it does not have to be like that.

There is still great joy to be found in parenting, caring and educating in the early years and I have attempted to incorporate many examples of children's thinking and language, as well as photos and pieces of their work. One aim of this book is to enthuse readers, whatever their roles and responsibilities for young children, so that they return refreshed to their hugely important work with young children and treat it as if it were the best possible kind of play. We should strive to find and hang on to the 'wow factor' in all our dealings with young children; I mean by this always being ready to be impressed, amazed and enchanted by them. This is not a 'soft' or romantic option, for it takes courage, intelligence and creativity to understand and respond appropriately to children and take on the role of being challenging partners in their learning.

I have often been told that the best way to read a text is to bring one's own questions to it and make reading a kind of interrogation of the text. Perhaps it will help you to know what questions I had in mind as I wrote this text:

- What might an appropriate language curriculum for the early years look like?
- Are the current national frameworks and requirements likely to nurture successful literacy in the early and later years?
- What can we learn from different approaches and beliefs about early education and the teaching of language and literacy?
- What can parents, carers, educators and local communities do to support language development in the early years?

This book is not in the business of providing foolproof answers, but it does hope to provoke a lot more questions and a lot more thinking about language, literature and literacy.

1

Great communicators

The setting is a fine spring evening in a Cornish seaside town. A young couple with a child of around 12 to 15 months of age are sitting by the harbour. The child's buggy has been positioned as close as possible to the railings along the harbour wall and the child is leaning forward and gazing intently down at the rising tide, pointing at the lapping water, feet kicking excitedly, shouting 'sea', 'sea', 'sea'. The mother responds by saying 'Yes, it's the sea' several times.

This chapter focuses on:

- brainy babies, communication and minds;
- major developments in early language;
- supporting young communicators.

It is all too easy to assume that an interest in children's language development must start with an interest in words and how children learn to use them. In the course of history many parents and scholars have believed just that and waited impatiently for infants to say their first words. Some legends suggest that an emperor with a taste for language study actually conducted an experiment to see if the first words of some unfortunate babies he had kept in isolation would be Latin! Even modern albums of the 'our baby' type, used for recording a child's development, usually include a page for 'first words'. But if we really do wish to understand more about language and support its development in childhood, we need to start much earlier: we have to look at what is going on in the first hours and days after birth and not be misled by the excitement of words.

Creating brainy babies

Studies of how the brain develops, known as neuroscience, confirm the importance of the first year or so of life. At birth the brain is highly adaptable and rich in potential but its millions of brain cells (neurons) are not connected by the all-important neural pathways (synapses) that make satisfactory emotional development and complex thinking possible. The crucial linking-up is triggered by daily experiences of being touched, cuddled, fed, moved around, sung and talked to, played with and generally stimulated.

Babies' brains are literally created in sociable and enjoyable relationships with their first carers. The necessary stimulation for growing a social brain (Gerhardt 2004) is learning in companionship from ordinary sensory and sociable experiences in families and small groups (Trevarthen 2002). This is not a matter of hot-housing babies, but providing consistent care, warm and appropriate responses and varied experiences of touching, tasting, listening, seeing and moving.

Communicating

For generations parents and carers have sensed that their newborn infants are attentive, playful and friendly, and modern research now supports such intuitions with clear evidence. It would seem that babies are great communicators from birth and have a range of pre-programmed abilities (instincts) that enable them to form close relationships with their carers. For example, babies prefer to look at human faces and eyes and pay attention to human voices. They actually spend remarkably long periods of time just gazing into the eyes of their carers (Schaffer 1977; Stern 1977). The recipients of this adoration are normally entranced and respond by smiling, nodding, talking and stroking the child's face, especially the cheeks, chin and lips. To an observer this behaviour can look remarkably like a real conversation, with turns taken to speak and gaps left for the 'speechless' baby to slot in comments. The adult partner behaves 'as if' this were a conversation and the slightest blink, squeak or squirm from the child is interpreted as a meaningful communication. But the infant partner is also very discriminating and will only give this level of attention to people. Although moving objects are tracked and watched, it is familiar adults who are usually treated to smiles, speech-like lip movements and arm waving (Trevarthen 1993). Furthermore, babies can set the pace for communications, making eye contact when they are feeling alert and sociable and dropping their gaze when they no longer wish to play this early language game. All these abilities are illustrated in Figure 1.1, as 12-week-old Dylan enjoys a relaxed conversation on the bed with his father. The photo has captured the remarkable mirror image between the partners: their eyes are locked in a mutual gaze and even the shaping of their lips and the opening of their mouths are synchronized. The movement of Dylan's right arm suggests that he is conducting the pace and duration of this particular conversation.

Continuing research into the sociability and communication skills of babies has demonstrated that they can imitate some interesting adult behaviours within minutes of birth (Trevarthen 1993). The list of actions imitated includes mouth-opening, tongue-poking, eye-blinking, eyebrow-raising, sad and happy expressions and hand opening and closing. Perhaps it is not too fanciful to see these actions as crucial ones in the life of a social being who will live in groups, small and large, and communicate face to face by means of voice, expressions and gestures. We cannot dismiss these earliest acts of communication as insignificant flukes; clearly they are pre-programmed (in the genes) and therefore of some survival value to our species. Furthermore, adult carers solemnly imitate their babies and go along with the agendas they set. All this has been observed

Figure 1.1 Dylan (12 weeks) and dad communicating.

in recent years by professionals as varied as anthropologists, psychologists, linguists and educators, and the fascinating business of baby-watching has attracted popular attention too (Morris 1991; Murray and Andrews 2000). There appears to be general agreement that early communication between babies and carers is a non-verbal form of 'getting in touch' with another person and crucial in the development of language, as well as of understanding and sympathy with others, and of social skills, cooperation and play.

Keep me in mind

The significance of this kind of learning in companionship (Trevarthen 2002) is now fully recognized and has become a major theory in current studies of child development, cognition and psychology (Saxe and Baron-Cohen 2007). It is known as theory of mind (TOM) and explores the ways in which babies' earliest social interactions with their carers build their understanding that other persons have emotions, motives and intentions and, therefore, their responses can be relied on and anticipated. This is not just a useful factor in playing games of peep-boo; it is central to the infant's sense of security and developing self-esteem. The first step in understanding the minds of others is for an infant to be able to feel held in mind by a loving and reliable carer. Carers who are tuned in to their babies are able to build a sense of attachment with them and this is the foundation of sound emotional development and mental health.

In their earliest communications with a human partner babies learn about themselves and how others see them. As they gaze into the eyes of their carers they see a mirror image of themselves and the responses of carers indicate how unique, human and loveable their infants are. This mirroring (Winnicott 1971), if it is a good experience, is the foundation of the child's own self-esteem and ability to love and inspire affection, and is yet another indicator of the significance of this period in a child's development when powerful communications take place without words.

Communicating babies and their carers do not live in vacuum packs and the worlds of particular cultures and communities shape their gestures, expressions, movements, talk and songs, so that from the start a baby enters a culture as well as a language. The basic patterns and timetable of language development are universal, but the fine details of gesture, talk, song and traditional care and beliefs about infants are as varied as the languages children learn. This is an important reminder that the roles of carers, families and cultural communities will always be of great significance in children's linguistic, intellectual and social development. Children do not just learn a language, they learn a way of life.

The kind of communication discussed so far is described by linguists as 'non-verbal communication': it helps to prepare babies for speech and underpins our use of spoken language for the rest of our lives. This word-less communication can also develop into sophisticated signing systems for the deaf, as well as complex signalling systems for activities as different as dance and mime, racecourse betting and aircraft landing control. The main characteristics of non-verbal communication in infancy are:

Non-verbal communication

- Face-to-face intimacy.
- Strong feelings (from warm affection to rage and frustration).
- Very dramatic use of facial expressions, especially eyes and eyebrows, mouth, lips and tongue.
- Whole body movements (including dancing, for example), head nodding and shaking, arm and hand gestures.
- The use of 'mouth sounds' like clicks, whistles, hums, 'raspberries' and loud 'boos'.

The last set of characteristics may seem a little bizarre, but we all make use of 'tuts', grunts, 'mms' and even whistles in our talk, especially on the telephone when we have to keep in touch with our invisible talk partner. In the early days of infant communication, imitating these exaggerated mouth sounds may help the baby to practise a whole range of sounds used in the eventual production of words, but we should also note that such sounds may be funny, outrageous and even rude. Right from the start there is a strong current of playfulness, mucking about and teasing in communication – and babies do as much of the mucking about as do their carers (Reddy 1991; Trevarthen 1993). This teasing is a kind of fib-bing, or playful deception, and is thought by some linguists to explain partly how language originated. In group life it was (and still is) important to be able to influence others, guess what was in their minds, and even 'change their minds'. Apparently the great apes, our nearest animal rela-tives, are 'extremely skilled deceivers' (Aitchison 1997: 26) – especially the chimpanzees – but for purely selfish reasons often connected with food. Human beings, however, can choose to tell a lie that is kind rather than brutally honest, and have turned fibbing into games (see Chapter 2) and 'telling tales' into an art form (see Chapter 3).

Finding the words

First words, when they come, do not spring perfectly formed after months of silence. As examples of meaningful sounds, they emerge from babbling, which has been strongly influenced by the sounds of the language, or languages, used constantly with and around the child. As understandable and regularly used labels for people, objects, feelings and events, they can be traced back to the early months of non-verbal communication, when babies develop recognizable 'sounds' for significant people, toys and noisily impressive objects like lorries and aeroplanes. These personal labels evolved by an infant may start out as a 'gaa' or 'brr' but they gradually move closer to the standard words used in the home and speech community (Halliday 1975). In the course of this development they are often 'stretched' in their use by the child so that they can cover a whole range of similar events or ideas. For example, the sound or word for 'car' may be used for lorries, shopping trolleys and lifts; the early word for a significant male carer or parent may be used for any man seen in the street or on the local bus.

This gradual building up of a collection of important words for things is greatly helped by the behaviour of carers who communicate with babies and play the sorts of game that involve highly predictable routines with their own special sounds and words. For example, simply giving and taking things and saying 'please' and 'thank you', or waving and saying 'bye-bye', or pointing at and naming things in homes, streets, magazines, catalogues, picture books and on the television screen. All these important language games really get things going, but words are not just any old random sounds and identifying the first words of immature speakers is not easy (after all, they will have difficulty forming certain sounds for some years in early childhood). Because of this, modern linguists, unlike proud parents and carers, have a set of criteria for what is really a 'first word':

The first word

- It is used spontaneously by the child.
- It is used regularly in the same activity or context.
- It is identified by the carer.

The emphasis on spontaneous use is important because with first words we are looking for evidence of the child's ability to identify and attempt to share meanings by using words – we are not interested in the skills of a well-trained parrot! The best evidence for meaningful word use is the child's reusing of the word in appropriate and similar situations. Treating the carer as the expert who can recognize and identify these first words is essential because only a regular carer has intimate knowledge of the child, as well as detailed knowledge of the contexts in which early words emerge.

The expertise of carers and the contexts in which children use their first words are interesting features of early language learning. Many studies of first words have been conducted and later published by linguists working with their own children – or their grandchildren (Engel and Whitehead 1993) – because carers are best placed to understand their children and their settings. This very powerful insider knowledge has revealed, among other things, that first words start as personal but highly consistent sounds (Halliday 1975); that first words are vivid records of the home life, culture and experiences of children; and that toddlers continue to practise language – especially new sounds, rhymes and words – on their own before falling asleep (Weir 1962; Nelson 1989).

Children's first words indicate how they are sorting out and making sense of their particular worlds and they also provide a guide to what really matters to them. When collections of first words are analysed it soon becomes clear that they can be grouped under such headings as: members of the family, daily routines, food, vehicles, toys and pets (Whitehead 1990). Clearly, people, food, animals and possessions are of great importance to babies and their obvious attractions drive the infants' search for labels. Having the right words for people and things is an almost fool-proof way of getting others to help you get hold of, or stay close to, good things.

Also found among the first words are some simple instructions and requests such as 'up', 'walk', 'out', 'gone' and those really important little words in any language, 'yes' and 'no' (or their linguistic equivalents). All these kinds of words enable a small and fairly immobile person to manage other people, get help and make personal needs and feelings felt. During this 'first words' phase of language development it is obvious to parents, carers and professional linguists that children's single words frequently stand for quite complex sets of meanings, communications and instructions. A word like 'dirty' can in certain situations mean 'my hands are dirty', 'are you putting my paint-splashed T-shirt in the washing machine?' or 'I've dropped my apple on the floor'. Only the carer who is with the child at the time can understand and respond appropriately to such one-word utterances – and may still get them wrong! Human communication is always a sensitive and risky business and single words can only do so much.

In order to unlock more of the power of language the young communicator must put words together in meaningful and unique combinations.

The power of language

Once young children begin to combine words together it is even more obvious that they are thinking for themselves and have some powerful understanding about how languages work. The evidence for these big claims can be found in the children's unique language creations that cannot have been imitated from adults and older children. We are likely to hear such requests as 'door uppy' (open the door) and 'no doing daddy' (don't do it daddy), and older infants go on to create new verbs out of nouns, as in 'lawning' (mowing the lawn) and 'I seat-belted myself' (putting on a seat-belt). Professional linguists get very excited about these examples (although other people often dismiss them as 'funny things children say') because they are evidence that all children are born with an innate ability to understand and produce appropriate and meaningful language (Chomsky 1957; Aitchison 1989; Pinker 1994). In fact, this remarkable ability to combine words together so that they make sense is grammar in action and indicates that a child is capable of thought, as well as being able to socialize and influence others.

Professional linguists describe 'grammars' in terms of the things they enable us to do with language and the two highly significant functions of language are: getting things done – especially with the help of others – and commenting and reflecting on the world (Halliday 1975). Young children certainly use their emerging skills as speakers in order to get carers and others to do things for them ('chair uppy': lift me onto the chair), and they also make statements that suggest they can observe the world and comment on what happens ('no more miaow', said as the cat leaves the room). It is worth emphasizing that these early word combinations are evidence of thought, and of an innate ability to share and communicate meanings. Many people are convinced that language is for communication and socializing, which it is, but they overlook its role in our thinking and memory. Yet there is powerful research evidence, as well as common sense, to tell us that language creates and extends our ability to think about abstract and complicated ideas such as 'trust' and 'freedom', or things that are distant in time and space (dinosaurs; Australia; last week's visit to the cinema; my first taste of ice cream), as well as the entirely invented and non-existent 'little green creatures from Mars', Paddington Bear and Jane Eyre.

These are examples of language as a symbolic system; that is, a way of letting words stand for things, ideas and experiences even in their absence,

so that we can hold onto them and think about them. This is so cer
human thinking that in cases where disease or genetic damage im
prevent the development of speech and language other symbolic systems
must evolve. The signing and touching 'languages' used by the deaf and
the blind provide ways of sorting, ordering, recalling and reflecting on experience as well as gaining the cooperation of others. In early childhood the
developmental patterns of affected children may show some personal and
some general variations. The emergence of grammatical understanding
will be in the normal range because it is pre-programmed and universal,
but early word acquisition may show some delay (Harris 1992) because
it is triggered and enriched by all the social and cultural naming and labelling games played with babies. It is important that infants who do have
some form of sensory impairment have endless opportunities to touch,
feel, move rhythmically, sign and name all the people, objects, materials
and animals in their environments. We can still learn a great deal from the
inspired teacher who placed the hands of the blind and deaf Helen Keller
under a gushing water pump and constantly wrote the letter signs w-a-t-
e-r on the child's palms as the water poured over them. Such support was
left almost too late for Helen Keller who had to retrieve years of loneliness
and frustration, but every impaired infant can be helped from the start
with a range of stimulating sensory experiences linked to words or signs.
In recent years there has been considerable interest in the role that signing
can play in the communicative development of hearing children and many
informal groups have been set up. These tend to be for toddlers under the
age of 2, accompanied by their carers, and they are introduced to a range
of basic British Sign Language (BSL) signs through the medium of songs
and rhymes.

In many ways learning languages never stops: we all increase our stock
of words and continue to pick up the latest technical terms and fashion-
able slang of our groups and cultures. Many children start with more
than one language, particularly in multilingual societies, or go on to acquire a second and third language at an early age. Some adults learn a
new language for professional or social reasons, even to enhance their
holidays in foreign countries, and schools in most societies are required
to teach one or more other languages. The process of becoming literate
and learning the written system of a language is also part of language
learning, as is the skilled way in which we all adjust our language (di-
alect) and our pronunciation (accent) according to particular situations
and audiences. But the earliest stages of learning to speak in childhood
hold a great fascination for most adults who work with children and/or
raise their own families, and some kind of developmental timetable is
often asked for. However, such timetables can be rather dangerous if

they are taken too seriously and interpreted with rigidity. So here, with that health warning, is a rough guide to major developments in early language.

Major developments in early language

- From birth, watching, listening, crying, squealing, gurgling and cooing at around 8 weeks.
- From around 6 months, babbling and vocalizing. From 9 to 12 months, more varied pitch, rhythm and tone. Sounds become increasingly like the sound patterns of the language(s) used by carers.
- Around 12 to 18 months the first words may be identified.
- From 18 months onwards the first word combinations appear. These may be unique two- and three-word patterns followed by simple sentences of three and four words, or more.
- Between 2 and 4 years there is a huge increase in vocabulary, more control over articulation and pronunciation and more complex language emerges. Language is used for many purposes: to get things done, ask questions, comment on events, feelings and people, tell stories, speculate and argue.

Supporting young communicators

In conclusion, we need to be proud of young children's language, thinking and early literacy behaviours, and be able to defend a sensible descriptive view of languages. Grammar is not an undisciplined free-for-all, but describes the rules of a language operating on at least three levels concerned with:

- the organization and patterns of *sounds* (known as phonology);
- the meaningful *combination of words* (known as syntax);
- the *meanings* of words and groups of words (known as semantics).

A fourth level, the *vocabulary* or stock of words in a language (known as lexis), is often included in grammatical descriptions.

This description of several levels of grammatical rules highlights the skill and complexity involved in the everyday use of language by any speakers and the remarkable achievements of young children in learning languages. However, this is not an easy guide to teaching grammar – in most cases these rules are far too complex for direct teaching – but it is a kind of ground plan for basing our approaches in the early years on children's love of language, their desire to communicate and their need to make sense of life and experiences. If simple rules are required, then we could do no better than suggest:

- Raising the status of *talk* and *communication*.
- Ensuring that any language use, spoken or written, is *appropriate for its purpose and situation*.
- Drawing children's attention to print everywhere and *making print exciting*.

Successful caring, parenting and educating is bound up with paying close and serious attention to young children and helping them to understand their world and manage themselves in it. But taking children seriously as people does not have to be grim and humourless – on the contrary, the best adult carers and educators are the most playful. The child watching the rising tide at the start of this chapter was already at the single-word naming stage of communication, but she (or he!) had been supported just enough to make talk about the sea possible: the buggy was as close as safety allowed to the edge of the harbour wall so that the child could peer down; time was made for uninterrupted watching; the child's recognition and naming of the sea was taken up by the mother and confirmed and expanded into a fuller statement. Above all, the sheer joy of watching the sea was communicated and shared. We can assume that this kind of communication had been repeated in other settings and circumstances many times before and had developed out of months of child and adult play, subtle body language, adult talk and shared communicative sounds and gestures.

We have to value all the non-verbal interactions that occur between infants and adults (or older children) in homes and group settings, create extra opportunities for them, and continue to value a wide range of non-verbal communications after spoken language is established. This will be particularly crucial for children whose first language is not English when they enter care and group settings, because they have to depend on picking up all the non-verbal communicative clues they can. The challenge this presents for the professional adults working with these young potential bilinguals can, however, lead to a wonderful freeing up and transforming of the procedures and curriculum in the setting.

Summary

Babies are active communicators from birth and in partnership with their carers they develop strong emotional attachments. At the same time, these experiences of communicating and socializing create the essential neural pathways in babies' brains. Language develops rapidly on these foundations of communication and emotional attachment, growing from cries and babbling to single words and simple utterances. The toddler uses language for an increasing range of purposes and adult carers have a continuing responsibility to be warmly supportive, challenging and enthusiastic language partners.

Provision and activities

The following will help to ensure rich linguistic beginnings:

- *People* Play, talk and just living with other people are the key activities at this stage. At home, parents, other family, siblings, childminders and nannies are the key provision. In group care settings, key persons and consistent carers for the youngest babies; a wider number of familiar adults for toddlers, as well as same-age peers (babies who are able to sit up enjoy the company of other babies).
- *Places* In group settings some small rooms and sheltered areas, inside and out, with cushions, carpeted areas and blankets to lie and sit on. In homes and group settings: safe unlockable cupboards, dens (tables with floor-length drapes/cloths over them) or full-length curtains to hide behind. Outside areas: garden houses, trees, bushes and improvised tents (blankets and sheets over bushes, tree branches and clothes-airers); fencing to peep through or imagine what lies on the other side.
- *Things to do* Face-to-face gazing, talking, gesturing, bouncing, singing, dancing, clapping; opportunities for listening and quiet watching (other children and adults, animals, moving trees, mobiles), looking out of windows, looking at pictures, books; signing, gesturing, finger rhymes and action songs; 'helping and talking' activities like food preparation, clearing up and domestic chores, bath times, getting dressed, gardening, shopping, walks and visits; opportunities to play with collections of natural and manufactured objects presented in 'treasure baskets' (Goldschmied and Jackson 2004) (e.g. wooden and metal spoons, fir-cones, shells, sponges, containers and lids, balls); also, saucepans and lids, rattles, squeakers, simple percussion instruments, wooden and plastic blocks (building bricks), soft toys and dolls; a small collection of picture, story, poetry and alphabet books with floor cushions, blankets and big comfortable chairs.
- *Things to talk about* All the above provide ample opportunities for communication and talk and the development of complex forms of thinking.

Further reading

Blakemore, S-J. and Frith, U. (2005) *The Learning Brain: Lessons for Education*. Oxford: Blackwell.

Gerhardt, S. (2004) *Why Love Matters: How Affection Shapes a Baby's Brain*. Hove: Routledge.

Gopnik, A., Meltzoff, A. and Kuhl, P. (1999) *How Babies Think: The Science of Childhood*. London: Weidenfeld & Nicolson.

Mortimer, H. (2007) *Listening to Children in their Early Years*. Stafford: QEd Publications/Stockton Borough Council.

Murray, L. and Andrews, L. (2000) *The Social Baby: Understanding Babies' Communication from Birth*. Richmond: The Children's Project.

Tizard, B. and Hughes, M. (2002) *Young Children Learning*, 2nd edn. Oxford: Blackwell.

Wells, G. (1987) *The Meaning Makers: Children Learning Language and Using Language to Learn*. Sevenoaks: Hodder & Stoughton.

Whitehead, M. (2007) *Developing Language and Literacy with Young Children*, 3rd edn. London: Paul Chapman.

Play and language

The family are having dinner and 7-year-old Daniel overhears his grandfather saying to another adult, in an aggrieved tone, 'I'm doing my best'. Daniel glances mischievously at his sister and then says with exaggerated politeness to his grandfather, 'Did you say "I've ruined my vest"?'. At this point both children giggle helplessly.

This chapter focuses on:

- play, players and the Early Years Foundation Stage (EYFS) in England;
- play with language;
- phonics, legislation and literacy;
- supporting play with language.

Contradictory as it may seem, this chapter attempts to get serious about play and looks more closely at what is going on when young children muck about with whoever, or whatever, comes to hand. Perhaps we recall a baby who has wriggled under its blankets and inadvertently caused the rattles strung across its pram or crib to shake musically. In no time the infant is engrossed in finding ways of moving so that the rattles shake on demand and this can soon lead to bashing them with energetic sweeps of the hands. An older infant who is more mobile will discover that bunches of keys can be shaken to produce sounds; saucepans can be banged and clashed, 'drunk' from in a pretend way, or even worn as hats! Toddlers will talk to soft toys, picture books and cushions, or pretend to be windscreen wipers, monsters and crying babies. Groups of 3- and 4-year-olds will create elaborate dramas about such themes as space, holidays, weddings, hospitals and jungles, and begin to delight in nonsense words, verses and slightly rude ideas and language. And the safe and confident 6- or 7-year-old can make fun of granddad by echoing the rhyme and the rhythm of his speech, but changing the words, as Daniel did. This game with language is played by children whenever songs, hymns, commercial jingles or television theme tunes are given newer and ruder words: 'Neighbours, pick your nose and taste the flavours' (from a south-east London Reception class).

If we try to distance ourselves from these very ordinary examples of playful behaviour in infancy and early childhood by looking at them as if for the first time, we may be struck by their remarkable features. So let us imagine what an observer from Mars would record about the young human:

- Things are not always what they seem: a cushion can be a baby; a dark corner can be a cave; a child can be a cat; and a child who is misrepresenting an adult's words may be praised.
- Things can be changed: a cooking pot is a headdress, a cup for non-existent drink and a percussion instrument; a simple chair can also be used as a ladder or a launch pad for flying leaps.
- Things can be controlled: accidental sound effects can soon be repeated to order by a baby who finds ways to move rattles and mobiles; the anger of adults can be managed and dispersed by jokes and laughter; adult attention and help can be organized by infants using cries, smiles and words.
- Things can be repeated and practised: infants repeat movements that bring pleasure or new sensations; certain stories, songs and words are listened to and said again and again by young children; children also imitate the behaviours and appearance of some animals, people and objects.

Our Martian observer would have to conclude that these goings-on must be of great significance for the human species and would not be surprised to learn that the study of many kinds of playful behaviour is an important ingredient in modern academic work in psychology, linguistics and literacy. We might also expect our galactic visitor to ask to see the curriculum arrangements for such an important activity as play in our education systems!

Play and the Early Years Foundation Stage (EYFS)

There has been a long tradition of explaining play, but in western and Anglo-Saxon cultures it has tended to be regarded as a bad habit that has to be exposed and perhaps excused. This has persisted and coloured modern attitudes to young children and to their schooling, and we must all be aware of the distinctions made between play and work in most adults' minds. This narrow view of play has now been challenged by recent legislation in England, Wales and Scotland. The English EYFS (DfES 2007a) applies to the care and education of all children from birth to 5 years of age and became statutory from 1 September 2008. The relationship between play and learning is one of the principles underlying the guidance for the EYFS. This principle is explained in a section on 'Play and Exploration' (PiP Card 4) stating that, 'In their play children learn at their highest level'. References are made to the significance of play for brain development, imagination and the growth of confidence and competence. The importance of play, talk and interaction with sensitive adults who engage children in 'sustained shared thinking' about their ideas, decisions and questions is seen as central to quality learning in the early years (Siraj-Blatchford et al. 2002; Sylva et al. 2004). These views on play in stimulating environments appear to have also influenced the government's Children's Plan published at the end of 2007 (DCSF). This document asserts that children need to enjoy their childhoods and promises more new playgrounds, a play strategy (DCSF 2008) that explains the significance of play for children's learning and well-being and a primary review to look at play-based learning in the early primary years (5–8?). This proposed primary review should not be confused with the ongoing independent Primary Review based at Cambridge University that has already reported on the need for more talk in primary classrooms and more pretend play in the early years (www.primaryreview.org.uk). The effectiveness of this upsurge of interest in play will depend on its implementation by early years and primary practitioners who have the knowledge, skills and experience to support play and young players.

Play and players

Traditional views of play tended to describe and explain what purposes it might serve from the biological perspective of the species, and so the suggestions covered such possibilities as using up excess energy, repeating some developmental features of human evolution, or practising skills that would be essential to adult life. Modern approaches look more closely at the individual who is playing and try to capture the flavour of what it feels like to be playing, as well as the purposes of the player. There is some room in such studies for the older concerns with practising skills and most contemporary scholars emphasize the long and vulnerable childhood of the human individual and the need for close and mutually satisfying relationships with carers (Bruner 1976). Perhaps the major differences in modern approaches are, first, the emphasis that is put on the child as an active player from birth who initiates and even choreographs the dance of communication and play with carers (Reddy 1991; Trevarthen 1993). Second, a keen awareness of the role of play in infant communication skills and early language, and in a most significant form of human thinking – the symbolic.

These are very complex ideas, and an everyday example might help:

> The tube train I am travelling on stops at a station and an Asian couple with a toddler in a buggy get on (I can only guess that the child is around 18 months old). The train is fairly crowded and the man stands while the woman sits and places the buggy so that the child can face the man. The little girl fixes her carer with a very 'smiley' gaze and begins to go through a remarkable and silent performance: first she waves her right hand in a vertical up and down gesture, the man smiles and responds with the same wave. Next the child waves in a horizontal left–right, right–left movement and the man responds by copying this. The next trick in the little girl's repertoire is to slowly drop her head onto first one shoulder and then the other, all the while maintaining steady eye contact with her male carer. Clearly these intimate and endearing communication games have been played and developed over some time, but the child is not entirely unaware of the people around her in the train. Another female passenger begins to wave back to the child and tries to catch her eye and this eventually breaks the spell between child and carer. At this point the child is both fascinated, wary and shy and resorts to peeping at the stranger from under the basket on the handles of the buggy and then twisting round completely to gain eye contact and reassurance from her female carer.

In this incident we see the child confidently in charge of starting and leading all the little communication games with her carers. In contrast, we also see how she is confused and wary when a stranger breaks in on the performance. The gestures and body language are examples of human symbolic behaviour and, like adult handshakes, nods and smiles, they stand for particular meanings in particular communities. Symbols always stand for something: they are more than they seem because they carry meanings.

Symbolic thinking is a powerful and economic way of thinking and understanding almost anything and is essential when we need to think about difficult and abstract ideas that cannot be touched, tasted or pointed to – ideas like 'loyalty' or 'distance', for example. We need some kinds of shared symbol if we are to share with others our feelings and ideas – just as the toddler on the noisy and crowded tube train needed to assert her security and identity by rehearsing her rituals of attachment with her carer. We also need the symbolic systems of languages, pictures, movements, and so on if we are to communicate about what is far away, in the past, or total fantasy. The solution to these difficulties is to let something – the symbol – stand for ideas, objects, feelings, events, and so on. And symbols can be many things: the words of a language, a baby's special sound for a toy or person, a gesture, a uniform, a bunch of flowers, a drawing, a religious ceremony or a national anthem. Our whole lives are spent creating, using and responding to symbols and our babies begin the process at (or soon after) birth, when they fill their relationships with carers and objects with emotion and feeling, so that blankets, breasts or feeding bottles are more than objects – they are security, relationships, identity and a sense of worth (Winnicott 1971). It is in this way and at this early stage that our names and the sounds of our languages take on a special life and feeling for us. Similarly, wider experiences increase the symbolic resources and thinking of young children so that soft toys are cuddled and loved, the shadowy space under the table becomes a cave and a long stick can easily be a horse to ride. An early introduction to stories and rhymes will extend the experiences and thinking of children by offering new symbols to use in the form of fictional characters, activities and situations (see Chapter 3).

Play in childhood and in adult life creates a kind of space and time where we can try things out without having to match up to external notions of correctness and can take risks. During play we can get to grips with things that matter to us alone, build new relationships with other people and even take time out to do nothing at all. Players of any age are typically engrossed in their play and although we often hear that play must be defined as pleasure or enjoyment, this should not be taken to mean that smiles and laughter accompany all play. Play can be deeply thoughtful and challenging, or it may explore emotions such as anger, pity and sadness. Careful observations of young children playing reveal that they struggle to build a tower of bricks, try to divert waves into a sandcastle's moat, play at being dead (Almon 1997) and even organize funerals (Lofdahl 2005). What we can say about young players is that they have set their own tasks and challenges, are 'supposing' about the chances of life, and finding useful symbols to play and think with. They are also investigating their world, being creative and flexible, and learning. Because how they feel about the things they are doing is central to play, they are also developing emotionally. This latter point is now taken very seriously by modern psychologists who deplore the damage done to children by narrowly academic kinds of education that originated in the nineteenth century and are a hopelessly inadequate preparation for twenty-first century thinkers (Gardner 1991; Goleman 1995; Claxton 1997). The issue here is the danger of missing out on children's extraordinary potential for all kinds of thinking and feeling if families, early years group settings and schools ignore or undervalue play and the development of the full range of human intelligences. Intelligence is not just a single ability to solve problems by mathematical logic – there is also musical, linguistic, bodily, artistic and interpersonal intelligence, to name but a few.

Play with language

Language and play share several characteristics: both use symbols to stand for a range of ideas, feelings and experiences; both are reflections of human thinking and also creators of new thoughts; both are part of our genetic make-up. Language is also one of our first playthings in infancy and remains an important play area for us, long after we have given up mud pies, rattles and dolls. The following examples are focused on early childhood but will indicate the persistence of play with language into adulthood.

Play with language can be simplified for the purposes of discussion by dividing it into two broad aspects: play with the matter, or stuff, of language, and play with the meanings encoded, or expressed, in language. The stuff of language is sound and there is little doubt that very early language play begins when babies – often helped and copied by their carers – gurgle, blow 'raspberries' and bubbles, squeal, grunt and babble. Babbling is a form of rhythmic early mouth play with the sounds of what will become a language, and is usually accompanied by bouncing, rocking and arm and leg pulsing movements. The pleasure and ease of babbling, repeating the same sounds in the same parts of the mouth and throat, still satisfy us long after we have given up babbling. So we sing 'la-la-la' or 'doo-bee-doo' to our favourite tunes, chant rhythmically at sports matches, rallies and demonstrations, or admire the scat singing of jazz musicians. As children mature and have wider social experiences they learn to chant over and over again the simple tongue-twisters, taunts street raps of their communities. Such favourites as 'she sells sea shells on the sea shore' and 'cowardy, cowardy, custard' are rather thin on deep meanings but are rich examples of repeated sound patterns and rhythms.

Children are very sensitive to rhyming sounds in their languages and it is no coincidence that the traditional literature of infancy and early childhood is rhyming verses, notably the nursery rhymes of the Anglo-Saxon cultures. Rhyme can be complex but a simple definition is the occurrence of matching or identical sounds in words or in the end sounds of lines of verse:

Humpty Dumpty
Sat on a wall
Humpty Dumpty
Had a great fall

If rhyme draws our attention to the end sounds of words, alliteration works by choosing identical or similar beginning sounds, as in tongue-twisters like 'Peter Piper picked a peck of pickled peppers'. Rhythm, rhyme and alliteration are the basic tools of the poet and the song-writer and they make it very easy to remember lines and whole verses. They would have been important memory aids in non-literate societies and they still work for pre-literate young children and busy adults who want to hang on to the words and rhythms of a favourite song or verse.

One other important form of play with the stuff of language is the simple pleasure of repeating favourite words or phrases over and over again. This can be a child's reaction to the beauty and strangeness of newly found words and I have memories of one small girl who was enchanted by the word 'strawberry' and shouted it aloud for days. Many adults still cling to childhood snippets, which may be reassuring but are no longer conveying literal meaning, as with phrases like, 'goodnight, God bless', or just 'bless you'. But the real culmination of all this play with the material of language is the art of poetry – yet poetry is far from being a series of enchanting sounds empty of meaning, and we need to look at play with the meanings of language.

Young children encounter new words all the time and although the meanings of many words are fairly obvious in the context in which they are met, we are sometimes made aware by a child's misunderstanding that we do use some ordinary words in extraordinary circumstances. This usually happens when words have taken on some extra symbolic functions and become metaphors; that is, we refer to complex and abstract matters 'as if' they were something commonplace and everyday. Perhaps my explanation has not 'hit the nail on the head' (a metaphor), but the following example may 'grab you' (another metaphor):

> The situation is a family picnic on a village green in the Norfolk Broads. Several exotic-looking ducks are asleep under the surrounding bushes and I remark to my 7-year-old grandson, Daniel, that they are 'ornamental' ducks introduced into Britain. A group of visitors arrive and feed the birds on the nearby river and our sleeping ducks wake promptly and move off to the river bank for their share. Daniel shouts excitedly, 'They're not ornamental, Marian. They're moving, they're moving!'

Clearly Daniel understood just one literal meaning for 'ornament' until I used the word metaphorically, and this is how the slow process of acquiring complex word meanings proceeds. Often an experience of this kind is followed by lots of playful and experimental trying-out of the new word meaning. A Russian scholar noted a little girl describing a piece of stale cake as 'middle aged' (Chukovsky 1963) and a 3-year-old of my acquaintance was wildly excited when he first heard the word 'trip' used to mean an outing of some kind. Up to then he had only used it to mean a fall, so he drove us all a little weary by staggering around giggling and elaborately pretending to trip over paving stones while shouting constantly: 'He's going on a trip today!'

The clowning reaction of this little boy reminds me that there is considerable research evidence from other cultures that children between the ages of 2 and 4 delight in nonsense and turning their newly-learned language upside down (Chukovsky 1963). This same research suggests that nonsense verse and silly jokes are very popular with young children because the craziness of it all helps them to sharpen their own grasp on reality and assert their own superiority to characters who go to sea in sieves or burn their mouths with cold porridge! One other very significant finding from Chukovsky's study was that attempts to suppress young children's playful and exploratory thinking and language use by imposing adult information and realism were totally ineffective. This should be remembered when early years provision and an appropriate curriculum are being planned.

lay way' to literacy and phonics

There was a fashion in the early decades of the last century to name reading schemes – which were usually phonics-based – as if they were pathways to rapturous joy and happiness, so little children skipped along 'gay' ways and 'radiant' ways to the promised land of literacy. My own small contribution to this tradition is to claim that children are more likely to become enthusiastically literate if play with the sounds and the literal and metaphorical meanings of language is taken seriously in the early years.

The whole issue of phonics and alphabet knowledge has received a great deal of publicity in recent years and families, carers and early years educators are under considerable pressure (some of it statutory) to follow misguided advice. This arises because so many people have a simplistic understanding of language, literacy and human thinking and believe that traditional phonics, which started by teaching one sound matched to one letter of the alphabet, can help with reading English – a language that happens not to be very consistent at the level of representing sounds. People will earnestly claim that they learnt to read this way, but they are clearly unaware of all the other experiences, complex skills and insights that came together as they learnt to read.

It is a fact that modern psychologists and linguists have studied young children's sensitivity to rhyme and alliteration, their knowledge of nursery rhymes and their recognition of letters of the alphabet. These researchers do not talk about traditional phonics as described above, and refer to their work as research into children's _phonological awareness_ and _alphabetic knowledge_. Their research suggests that pre-5s who have had considerable informal experience of sharing rhymes, songs, alphabets, picture books and daily routine talk with carers are already sensitized to language and literacy and likely to make an early start on reading (Bryant and Bradley 1985; Hasan 1989; Goswami and Bryant 1990). We do know that English-speaking children's reading development is closely connected with their knowledge of rhyme. In Chapter 1 there is a reference to research in the USA which gathered evidence that very young children alone in bed at night spontaneously practise new words and phrases and create their own sets of nonsensical and standard rhyming and alliterative words (Weir 1962; Nelson 1989). It is likely that this sensitivity to the rhythms and sound patterns of language is a universal feature of all cultures and their languages, as songs, poems, dances and music from around the world all indicate. So perhaps infants are 'wired' for rhyme and wordplay from the start (McArthur 1995) and we should concentrate on making the right connections with them and for them.

After Rose

The teaching of reading in England is now regulated by the recommendations of the Rose Review (DfES 2006). These recommendations have been incorporated into the statutory guidance for the EYFS and the Primary Literacy Framework. The approach is far from playful and requires systematic phonics to be taught to all children from the age of 5 in large class groups and at the same fast pace every day. The government standards website describes this, apparently without irony, as 'the simple view of reading', focused on word recognition and language comprehension. However, it is clear that word recognition is the main focus and comprehension is a later add-on feature. The guidance for practitioners, *Letters and Sounds* (DfES 2007b) sets out a six-phase teaching programme, week by week, and requires fast, systematic, repetitive and time-limited instruction.

Researchers, linguists and experienced educators have voiced considerable concern about this one-size-fits-all approach and the downward pressure it will exert on under-5s in EYFS settings. These experts point out that reading is far from 'simple', nor are the reading requirements for twenty-first-century literacy met by this nineteenth-century model! Research reports from the USA, where systematic phonics instruction has been dominant for some years, give support to these reservations (see Chapter 4). The sad history of older generations who failed to read with synthetic phonics in the nineteenth and twentieth centuries provides another kind of folk research evidence.

So can we still have fun with phonics? Perhaps we can, but a bit of playful subversion is necessary! One lovely example of this, put together by a group of expert practitioners, is called '*L*' *is for Sheep* (Featherstone 2006) and it is crammed full of play suggestions, games and fun activities. These include skipping and alphabet rhymes, I-spy, tongue-twisters, finding rhyming pairs and games that help with sound discrimination ('statues', 'traffic lights', 'dodgem cars'). Behind all this fun is a deep understanding of the significance of initial sounds and end rhymes in children's developing phonological awareness and early reading.

Supporting play with language

In this context of supporting early learning through play and experimentation, carers and educators have a responsibility to share with children all the many ways in which a community and a culture play with language. This is a simple matter of introducing young children to rhymes, songs, music and dance steps, sayings and proverbs, chants, advertising jingles, poems, jokes, puns and tongue-twisters, and so on. But this is not a matter of formal contracts to do 'play with language' once or twice a day for 10-minute sessions. It would be disastrous and as ineffective as giving newborns lessons in communication and language acquisition, or enrolling 1-year-olds for correct walking tuition! We know that play with language, particularly rhyming, is a powerful predictor of successful early literacy, but it is so just because it is part of what it means to be human and to think in linguistic and symbolic ways. The best pre-literacy lessons happen at home with parents when bathing infants and changing nappies, washing and peeling vegetables, singing and dancing to the tape/radio/television, making the beds or unloading a basket at the supermarket checkout (see below). Many of these activities can also be done in group settings and professional carers and educators should avoid using such oddities as 'sound tables' and phonic lists. The source of phonological knowledge is the human voice – people talking, singing and playing with languages (several if we are lucky).

Summary

Play is not only an intriguing feature of young children's development and early behaviour; it also appears in their early communication and language. Babies can be playful and teasing with their carers and as children develop their use of language, they also muck about with the sounds and the meanings of words, rhymes and stories. This urge to play with language can be a powerful impetus for early literacy as play with the sounds of words helps children make links between spoken sounds and their representation in letters and phonemes. The nurturing of this alphabetic and phonological awareness is a more useful start to literacy in the early years than formal, systematic, phonics instruction.

Provision and activities

- *People* Parents, carers and key persons to begin with, widening out to members of local families, communities and ethnic groups to encounter other languages, songs, rhymes and poetry; exposure to a range of accents and/or dialects; use of tapes, radio and television to broaden language listening and joining-in experiences; group settings can contact poets, storytellers and folk-singers for visits; regular contacts with other infants, toddlers and children – lots of play with language and learning new words, songs, rhymes, and so on, including the mildly naughty, happens in peer groups.

- *Places* Everywhere! (Homes, shops, buses, clinics, group settings, schools, playgrounds, parks.) The note on 'Places' at the end of Chapter 1 is equally appropriate here as small, sheltered and 'secret' spaces provide the safe and intimate settings we all need in order to take risks with play and with language.
- *Things to do*   All the activities listed under this heading at the end of Chapter 1 provide the essential beginnings of play with language.

Additional suggestions:

- *Bathing and nappy changing*   Child and carer blowing bubbles and making other mouth sounds (clicks, 'raspberries', humming); repeating names of child and carer, turning them into a rhythmic song, adding actual and nonsensical words that rhyme or are alliterative; doing the same for names of pets, nappies, bath toys, cream, clothes, and so on; accompanying these games and songs with bouncing, rocking, leg- and arm-waving, tickling, water-splashing, saying 'boo', whistling, finger-clicks.
- *Washing and peeling vegetables*   Adapt most of the above suggestions, singing rhythmically as the water runs into the bowl (simple chants such as 'we're washing carrots, we're washing carrots, they look like parrots, they look like parrots'); find another rhythmic chant for the peeling action; talk about what other fruits and vegetables are the same colour; list all favourite foods and all most disliked foods; if you find making up songs and chants difficult or a child is reluctant to do so, just sing nursery rhymes, folk and pop songs or commercial jingles. (My father sang cockney music-hall songs to me and so from an early age I could warble 'boiled beef and carrots' and 'my old man said follow the band' – some excellent rhymes and alliteration in this kind of material!)
- *Unloading a shopping basket*   Again, adapt all the above ideas. Items can be named as they come out of the basket, names can be repeated and alliteration and rhymes can be emphasized. This is a good chance to look at packaging, pictures, logos and letters. Pick out any initial letters that are the same as those of the child's name (this will soon lead to the child noting these letters all over packages, posters and buildings).
- *Enjoying the alphabet*   Start a small collection of published alphabet books; use paper or scrapbooks to begin to make alphabets for children, sticking on pictures, photos and children's drawings, but let the children choose the items (try to get away from 'A for apple, B for ball' and go for avocados and balti, couscous and dolmades). Personal alphabets can be made at home and in group settings. Think about a collection of nursery rhyme and poetry books to share on a daily basis; early years settings should convert their 'sound tables' into poetry tables and corners; record the child/children singing their favourite chants, songs,

rhymes, raps, poems, jokes, and so on (made up, traditional or modern) so that they are available for listening, signing and singing together sessions.

Play with language may seem silly and slightly subversive but it is intellectually stimulating for children and the foundation for literacy, phonological awareness and further language learning.

Further reading

Beard, R. (ed.) (1995) *Rhyme, Reading and Writing.* London: Hodder & Stoughton.

Bruce, T. and Spratt, J. (2008) *Essentials of Literacy from 0–7.* London: Sage Publications.

Chukovsky, K. (1963) *From Two to Five.* Berkeley, CA: University of California Press.

Goncu, A. and Gaskins, S. (eds) (2006) *Play and Development: Evolutionary, Sociocultural and Functional Perspectives.* NJ: Lawrence Erlbaum Associates.

Kalliala, M. (2006) *Play Culture in a Changing World.* Maidenhead: Open University Press.

Manning-Morton, J. and Thorp, M. (2003) *Key Times for Play: The First Three Years.* Maidenhead: Open University Press.

Paley, V.G. (1981) *Wally's Stories: Conversations in the Kindergarten.* Cambridge, MA: Harvard University Press.

Tovey, H. (2007) *Playing Outdoors: Spaces and Places, Risk and Challenge.* Maidenhead: Open University Press.

Once upon a time ...

> Once there was a magic circle in the forest and a giant lived inside.
> There was a boy and his sister walking into the forest. The giant tried
> to trick them because if you stepped inside the circle you turned into a
> spell. But he couldn't trick them so they went home and had supper.
>
> (Paley 1981: 66)

This chapter focuses on:

- stories and narratives;
- books and genres of literature;
- some book suggestions.

This storyteller is a 5-year-old black American boy called Wally who has taken to dictating a vast number of tales to his kindergarten teacher. Wally's stories seem to pour out of him in response to the daily events, people, feelings and puzzles of his life, at home and in the kindergarten. In this instance the story appears to have been inspired by a large circle painted on the kindergarten floor by the teacher, to create a simple stage for the children's dramatic improvisations. The remarkable thing about Wally's story is its familiar traditional ingredients: two vulnerable little children alone in the forest; the danger posed by a powerful giant; the courage and wisdom of the little children; and their safe return to home and supper.

This story is a significant achievement, but it is not an unusual one – stories, both mundane and fantastic, are made up and told by children of all ages, and by adolescents and adults. It seems that we are all born storytellers and our tales can be about our inner lives and emotions ('how we feel'), our current state of health ('how we are'), our religious beliefs and moral values ('what we believe'), our loyalties to families, cultures and nations ('who we are and where we come from'), or they can be re-workings of all the other stories we read, hear and see ('what we have learnt'). The prevalence of stories in our lives makes them of great interest to psychologists, psychiatrists, doctors, priests, politicians, journalists, artists and scientists. This can be rather a surprise to people who think that stories belong just to children, novelists, entertainers and English teachers, but there is a particular reason for early childhood educators and carers to take an interest in human story-making and story-sharing: it seems that we actually think – to a large extent – by using stories, and our memories are organized as a series of stories.

A simple demonstration of this is to ask people what sort of a day they have had; usually their response is in the form of a set of edited highlights from that day. The highlights seem to be selected because they matter to the teller, but also because the teller judges them to be of some interest to the listener. So our audience and our setting shape these personal stories and help the teller of any age to mull over events and feelings and judge their significance. In fact, so important are our stories to our thinking and our feelings that we tell them to ourselves, as if we had some kind of inner listener who was always there. Of course, very young children will not always tell their stories verbally, although they certainly talk to themselves a great deal. They act stories and dance them, they draw or paint them, mould them in mud, sand and clay, or even beat up a favourite teddy! So, what is a story?

What is a story?

A story is any number of happenings, real or imaginary, which have been organized so as to be told or shared in some form (words, songs, dances, ceremonies and rituals, cave paintings, and so on). The organizing system for stories is known as narrative and it provides a kind of backbone for all the stories we hear, see and tell. One very straightforward definition of narrative emphasizes the fact that it is always about 'telling': '*Someone telling someone else that something happened*' (Smith 1981: 228).

Here we have the most crucial and basic of all language activities. We hear it when a carer soothes a baby with a little story of how nice a trip to the clinic will be, or when a child in the nursery tells us about a mishap with the watering can. We also hear it in ancient legends, histories, poems and folk tales, as well as in modern novels, biographies and daily gossip. Yet, although we find these narratives everywhere, there is nothing random or sloppy about narrative tellings, and two essential characteristics identify a narrative: a concern with time and a concern with values.

A concern with time

A narrative is a sequence of events ordered in time, so that at its simplest we get the events of a story told in the order of their happening and linked by such language as 'and then ... and then ...'. Many carers will be familiar with a young child's account of a day at the playgroup that goes like this: 'I showed Mrs X my new gloves and then I played with the sand and then I went on the swing and then I sang "The Wheels on the Bus" and then it was home-time'. Teachers of older children in Key Stages 1 and 2 of the English National Curriculum will have noticed that this same basic narrative form is used by them in their early attempts at lengthy pieces of writing. It certainly is a wonderful device for spinning out a long oral story, a juicy piece of gossip or a lengthy written narrative. The long narrative in Appendix I was written over the 10 days of a Christmas holiday by siblings Daniel (7 years 1 month) and Natalie (9 years 11 months). It was inspired by imaginative play with a collection of toy bears and the main author was Daniel, but Natalie took over as scribe when Daniel tired, and she sometimes contributed to the plot. The division into chapters, the adventure theme and the 'blurb' on the back of the cover indicate how much the children were influenced by their knowledge of books and the patterns of the narratives they had heard and read since infancy.

The concern with time in narrative also indicates its links with the organization and functioning of human memory: 'When I was three and Bailey four, we had arrived in the musty little town, wearing tags on our wrists which instructed – "To Whom It May Concern" – that we were Marguerite and Bailey Johnson Jr., from Long Beach, California, en route to Stamps, Arkansas, c/o Mrs Annie Henderson' (Angelou 1984: 6). This kind of storytelling and writing is like a mental diary that is constantly added to and revised, and reminds us of who we are and what has happened to us. From the earliest years we have to know these things if we are to manage our lives and form satisfactory relationships with others.

A concern with values

Narrative is just as much concerned with human values as with time and this brings out the issue of selection and choice of what to tell and what to leave out. This is as important for the hearer or reader as it is for the teller and stories are enjoyed for the clues they give about the values, attitudes and judgements of the narrator(s). We may not agree with the values in a narrative, but we do add them to our stock of knowledge about people and about the chances of life. How often have you summed up a bit of gossip, or a strange story from the media, with a folk saying such as 'There's nowt queerer than folk' – as my Lancastrian mother-in-law would say? Narrative is a very important method for speculating on life and human behaviour and is not restricted to great novels and plays, as familiar sayings, proverbs and gossip indicate. It is an essential tool for all of us, but especially so for young children who often feel confused and vulnerable and have to find out a lot about people and life in as short a time as possible.

Community narratives

Throughout our lives we use narrative selection, ordering, telling and evaluating to give patterns, meaning and predictability to what would otherwise be random sensations and happenings. The evidence for this comes from communities and cultural groups as well as from individual development. The narratives of whole communities are usually stories that explain the origins, beliefs, history and moral values of the group and they are familiar to most of us as myths, legends, folk tales, rhymes, proverbs and sayings. All these would once have been part of an oral (spoken) tradition existing long before the development and spread of writing and printing. Much of the traditional literature we share with young children – for example, nursery rhymes, lullabies, nonsense, folk and fairy tales – is really ancient and full of the accumulated wisdom of many generations. Hence, the little bits of folk warnings we may recall from childhood: 'it will all end in tears'; 'never cast a clout until the May is out'; 'you made your bed and you must lie on it'.

However, this wisdom is not entirely in the past and groups and cultures still continue to make sense of their lives and pass on their experiences to their children. We now do so less by word of mouth, and instead use the media, organized schooling, places of worship and popular entertainment. For young children, these community narratives are significant introductions to the shared beliefs, values and meanings of their cultures. Many of us are comfortable with such cultural symbols as Paddington Bear, Anansi and Cinderella for discussing behaviour and moral viewpoints, but there is evidence that young children are eager to make sense of the most puzzling media narratives. Television news bulletins have been found to preoccupy

2- to 5-year-olds in Australia, as their attempts to make sense of them with their own retellings indicate:

Sara, 5:   I saw that. Princess Diana crashed and she got squashed.
Bekky, 5:   When she was getting buried, she was in a thing [makes a square using her fingers] with flowers on top.
(Weddell and Copeland 1997: 1)

Community narratives must deal with both the terrible and the joyful happenings in life and very young children need to talk about and play at funerals and crashes, as well as superheroes, weddings and space monsters. They also need to create narratives about their own identity, relationships and feelings.

Personal narratives

Researchers make very strong claims about the importance of narrative in personal development. It has been described as a primary function of the mind (Hardy 1977) and a kind of 'brain fiction' (Gregory 1977). Brain fictions are all the possible strategies or scenarios that we try out 'in our heads' before risking real action. Telling ourselves stories about 'what may be the case' is an instance of what is more grandly known as 'forming hypotheses' and this makes human thinking very much like scientific behaviour.

We need to be aware that very young children are constantly finding themselves in the same situations as research scientists: they are frequently meeting new events and happenings and trying to create stories that predict the most likely outcomes and offer explanations. Scientists' stories or hypotheses advance human knowledge; children's stories enable them to survive and cope with life, as well as adding to their personal store of knowledge. Listen to Mollie who is 2 years and 11 months as she struggles to do the right things in kindergarten: '"I'm not too big to reach that", she says, trying to hang up her jacket. "But my already birthday is going to come now. Then I can be big to reach it"' (Paley 1986: 4). Or eavesdrop on some 7-year-olds investigating a pair of broken spectacles found in a box of historical objects:

Sharon: It could have been the old man's and when he died, something could have happened to them to get broke ... something could have fallen on them.
Claire: Well the Romans could have knocked his glasses off and cracked them.
Children: [Several] No.

Josh: The old man wouldn't be alive. The old man wasn't alive when the Romans were here.

Kath: He would have been 2000 years old.

(Hoodless 1996: 114)

The stories these children from nearly 3 to 7 years old are narrating help them to deal with abstract ideas and difficult problems, and provide them with theories of life that can be modified and improved in the light of experience and new information.

The first two chapters of this book have emphasized how carers first tell their infants little tales about their appearance, mannerisms and personalities, and how personal storytelling and language play develop in 2-year-olds. From this stage children increasingly use in their own narratives the cultural sayings, songs and stories that they are told, see on television or overhear. Such expressions as 'once upon a time' or 'there was once a baby who got lost' or 'they all lived happily ever after' remind us that young storytellers are already beginning to sound more like books and have in fact begun to use orally the language of literacy. This really is one of the true basics of literacy. Babies and young children who hear plenty of oral stories and stories from books and television, and share in meaningful talk with adults and other children, become tuned in to the broad patterns of stories and the language and ways of thinking found in our written systems.

A *curriculum is a story*

This chapter began with Wally telling a story about the latest event in his kindergarten class, but it would not be correct to think that his narrative skills were just an accidental bonus for his teacher. In fact the teacher, Vivian Gussin Paley, built her early years curriculum on the children's narrating activities. She did this by audio recording *all* the daily talk and narrating that went on, and used this material as her guide to the children's current interests and knowledge, their questions and curiosity, and the first signs of new interests and queries. Her analysis of the children's daily narratives shaped her forward planning of activities and provision, as well as giving her insights into the children's individual all-round development and enabling her to make appropriate interventions and provide the right kind of support. She also reflected deeply on her own role and the purposes of early years education as she listened to the stories her children were telling.

Wally and the big painted circle incident tell us that mutually respectful talk between children and between adults and children, as well as story, rhyme, poetry, plays and dramatic re-enactments were the core of this particular narrative curriculum. But any curriculum is a kind of story, although it may not be as supportive of young children's learning as the Paley variety. A curriculum is a small selection, or story, chosen from all the thousands of possible things we could tell our children from our accumulated knowledge and experience. As such, like any narrative, it reveals a great deal about what a particular human group values and cannot bear to leave to chance in the passing on of information, beliefs and attitudes to the next generation. Our curriculum choices also show what we think will be absolutely essential for the survival and prosperity of our children, so for the last few hundred years developed countries have emphasized literacy and numeracy in any type of organized schooling, but not fishing, hunting and the building of simple shelters. Of course these skills may still be valued and taught by some families, clubs and groups.

The dominant curriculum stories in contemporary British schools and early years settings are about literacy and numeracy, along with narratives of our history (very selective and partial), plus some tales of the natural world and the human environment. This is an important reminder for all who work with young children – particularly in school settings at Key Stage 1 and the start of Key Stage 2 – that the only satisfactory way for children to understand the subjects of a national curriculum is through stories. We have to set the facts of science, technology, geography and history, for example, in the contexts of stories about how people live and solve problems now, in the past or in distant places. Similarly, we may tell stories of how animals survive and adapt, or introduce children to stories about the nature of materials and the universe we inhabit. This is not that difficult when we realize that human beings have always told stories that explained the pattern of the seasons, the shapes and locations of the star constellations and how the camel got his hump! What is difficult is having the courage to let the children work through and play with their own early explanatory stories – because they will certainly be creating them. Given time, respect and encouragement they will do what we all do: gradually modify their own personal theories with more and more of the 'facts' set down by tradition and experts. The alternative to this process of gradual assimilation is the unwise one of imposing facts on young children who, because they cannot make human sense of them and have nowhere to put them, dump them as soon as possible. This is unacceptable in terms of wasted educational opportunities and lives. Good early years carers and educators should always be telling manageable tales about the facts, from digital technology to multiple addition.

However, there is more to a curriculum than the facts, or subjects, we choose or are required to tell about. A curriculum includes 'all the learning opportunities' offered in a school or early years setting; 'all the behaviour that is encouraged or discouraged; the organisation and routines; the way adults, including parents, interact with the children' (EYCG 1992: 16). In other words, it is not just what you tell that counts, it is the way that you tell it. This involves the respect we show to children, the opportunities we provide for learners to make their own sense of our curriculum stories, and the chances they have to contribute to the curriculum. A backward-looking curriculum that only tells about some facts and values which suited a vanished world cannot help children to think and be socially and intellectually adaptable in the twenty-first century. Our children need a foundation early years curriculum that nurtures strong self-esteem, the ability to form loving relationships of many kinds, respect for the diversity and common humanity of others, a sense of social responsibility and the potential to think independently, creatively and flexibly. This may appear to be a very tall order but there are sound reasons to believe that a curriculum with play and literature at its core may deliver these good things (Heath 1997), *plus* the literacy and numeracy we all desire for our children.

Stories and literacy development

- Stories are a timeless and universal way of making sense of experience. They help us to impose order on random events. They also help us to understand the significance of what happens and they provide explanations for why people behave as they do.
- Stories are ways of thinking. They are a crucial resource for young thinkers as they go about their daily meaning-making activities.
- Stories and books are 'the basics' of literacy development. The most dangerous aspect of the new phonics orthodoxy is the advice to use only approved phonically regular texts and primers (reading schemes), rather than real books written by authors who tell tales about daily life and imaginary worlds.
- Stories (and books) come with an added linguistic bonus. They use language in all its varied rhythms and patterns, including such significant phonological features as alliteration and rhyme. Stories and books also offer rich examples of new, unusual and exciting vocabulary for the emergent reader.

The following section provides some advice for carers and educators who wish to begin, or develop further, the telling of tales to young children and goes on to discuss some important genres, or types, of literature and books for babies and young children.

Telling tales

Telling tales, as distinct from reading books to children, is an ancient and central human activity and still has the power to enchant audiences of any age. The ability to tell a story, no matter how short, is the educator's and carer's best life-saving kit! The tale can be a brief illustrative example of how not to 'wash' a lettuce, or about how big a dinosaur would have appeared if it stood in our local supermarket/park/high street. A spontaneous story can be made from a richly rambling account of what the teller's schooldays were like in rural Pakistan or Wales, or inner-city Baltimore or Belfast. Fantastic worlds of monsters, space aliens, little pigs, wizards, gods, monkeys, ghosts and abandoned orphans can also be conjured out of the air if we remember and share the tales we all heard in our own childhoods.

How to tell tales

The first instruction, and the most important, is: enjoy yourself! This means that you must enjoy the story you plan to tell and believe that it is really worth while; you should try to plan and rehearse your stories, including any little 'warm-ups' and any follow-up activities. Rehearsing a story means knowing where the crucial events in the plot occur and giving them plenty of emphasis. It also means knowing just how you will handle the climax and how you will end your tale. None of this involves learning 'off by heart' or being word perfect because every telling will be slightly different, in response to the setting, the audience (1 child; 20 children; in bed; in a playgroup; in a classroom) and the emotional mood. The things we need to plan ahead are the *bones* of the story – the flesh will grow with each telling.

The second instruction is: enjoy the language! Spoken language is at the heart of your telling and needs to be enjoyed for its actual sounds, rhythms and repetitions. Plan for lots of repeated phrases, no matter how daft! My grandchildren could never get enough of the ritual opening of every story my husband told them: 'When I was a lad, not much bigger than Leila is today . . . ' The joke was that Leila was their pet cat. Try to build in little jokes and nonsense, or snippets of songs, alliteration, rhymes, foreign words and playful mispronunciations, or whatever form of language play appeals to you and your children.

The third instruction is: enjoy the performance! Good storytelling is a performance and some acting skills are required, but it is more relaxing if you think of it as having the courage to make a fool of yourself. Your voice and your body are the means for communicating the story and they enable the child/children to understand and share it. This means using your voice in different ways to outline the plot events, set out the moral and emotional values of the narrative and describe the characters. All this can be done by changes of pitch and volume and a well-planned use of pauses. Characters can be identified by using different accents, styles and registers for them. Remember that regular eye contact with your listeners and your facial expressions, gestures, mimes and body language can also tell a great deal of the story and keep the listeners enthralled.

The fourth instruction is: help your listeners to enjoy themselves! Listeners need to feel secure and comfortable and should be reasonably close to the storyteller. In small groups and families this is not a problem with babies or small children in the carers' arms or snugly held on their laps, but large group settings and schools can also get round the difficulties by sitting children in a semicircle. Listeners must also be invited into the story and this is why well-planned opening routines, or the 'warm-ups' mentioned above, are so important. After all, a story is a turning away from everyday concerns and demands; it creates a space in which we contemplate life, explore new ideas and take some emotional risks – we may meet Wild Things, or get locked in the house! Some tellers like to make the break with everyday reality by singing a repeated phrase: 'It's story-time, it's story-time, sshh . . .' (Medlicott 1997). Some like to play a simple musical instrument like a pipe or a hand drum; others sing and use 'body music' (rhythmic hand-clapping, finger-clicking, thigh-slapping, knee-tapping, tongue-clicking, and so on). Other traditions include sitting in a special chair or wearing a special hat, shawl or jacket, and showing objects associated with the story (a magic pot, a shopping basket). All these ideas make storytelling time special, as well as holding the interest of the audience and guiding their responses. Furthermore, they can still be used and developed when reading stories from books is planned.

Final words: none of these special plans for storytelling should stop any of us from spontaneously telling a good tale when the moment is right, whether at bathtime, in the checkout queue, or over a family meal.

Books and literature in infancy and early childhood

Babies and books

Babies' books made of cloth, plastic or strong board are a kind of toy that has been around for a very long time and this reflects a widespread belief that babies born into a literate culture should have books as soon as possible – even in the bath. But books as books, rather than toys, have been shared with very young babies by some families for decades, although these families were usually academics, librarians and booksellers. What we might call 'bookish people'! Many of these families recorded and studied their infants' encounters with books and provide stunning evidence for the early literacy progress and emotional maturity of children who meet books when they are babies (White 1954; Butler 1979; Jones 1996; Whitehead 2002). The important point to be emphasized is that these families were *not* attempting to teach their babies to read in any formal way; they were parents and carers who loved books and literature themselves and wanted to share what they valued so highly with their children, almost literally from birth. We have to imagine the loving, intimate and secure settings in which these babies gazed at pictures, touched the print, gurgled responsively, bounced up and down with the rhythms of poetry, alliterative phrases and catchy rhymes, and probably sniffed at the smooth pages and covers of their favourite books, or sucked the corners. All these experiences would take place while the baby was calm after a feed, or securely held in a carer's arms, or feeling unsettled and needing comfort, or perhaps too wide awake to sleep, and in one rare case suffering great pain (Butler 1979). This strong emotional tone of comfort, well-being and security is never lost but becomes part of a reader's sense of total concentration on a book and temporary withdrawal from the demands of the world. Many adults and children 'switch off' from everything else when they read and prefer to read in such secluded places as the bath, in bed, under tables or behind curtains.

It seems that these special lessons about the pleasures of reading are best learnt in infancy, particularly if we want children to love books and reading rather than just learning to recognize words because someone else says they must. As a result of the growing awareness of the huge advantages and pleasures for carers and babies of book-sharing, attempts have been made to help many more families introduce books and story reading to their babies. This started with a carefully monitored pilot scheme in Birmingham that was organized through the local health visitors and the libraries (Wade and Moore 1993). 'Bookstart' packs containing a picture book, a poetry card, a poster and an invitation to join the local library were given free to the parents/carers of 300 9-month-old babies in the city. This project was not aimed just at bookish families and covered a wide ethnic, social and economic cross-section of the city. The questionnaires that the families filled in at the start of the scheme and after six months revealed that the joys of book-sharing soon affected the whole family and this included toddlers, older children and adults. In some cases it also led to joining the public library and buying books. A follow-up study of the original families showed that long-term enthusiasm for books had been sustained and the children spent longer periods of time with books and parents/carers (Wade and Moore 1996). A report about these children who started statutory schooling in the autumn of 1997 indicated that not only were they well ahead in speaking and listening and reading and writing, they were also ahead in mathematics (Wade and Moore 1997). It seems that really early experiences with books gave them good insights into numbers, shapes, space and measurement and the researchers attributed this to the counting games, rhymes, shapes and numbers in many children's books. This exciting work is now supported by the government and children's book publishers and extends to all areas of the UK. The original *Bookstart for Babies* pack has been joined by a *Bookstart Plus* pack for toddlers (around 18 months) and *My Bookstart Treasure Chest* for pre-school children. There is also a *Booktouch* pack for blind and partially sighted babies that includes two 'touch and feel' books and lots of useful advice for carers.

We may take away from this kind of research a greater respect for the abilities and potential of babies and the commitment and contributions of their parents and carers to the pleasures of early learning. Babies' earliest experiences with books may have a huge influence on their later attitudes to books and literature, and on their development as readers, writers and learners in the widest sense.

Traditional literature

Folk-fairy tales

At the start of this chapter 5-year-old Wally told a tale of a dark forest, magic spells, a dangerous giant and vulnerable little children. This story is a kind of summary of many of the traditional European folk and fairy tales we share with young children and, along with nursery rhymes, this material has become the literature of the early years of childhood. At first glance this seems strange because the content is very outdated, often cruel and frightening and full of beliefs we no longer accept. Yet the tales and the rhymes appear to be indestructible: they enthral young children; they have a strange hold over adults who remember them; artists and writers compete to produce their own versions; and modernized retellings of them abound.

What we now describe as fairy tales are in fact a group of ancient folk tales that were written down and made a little more polite and respectable for the French aristocracy's entertainment at the end of the eighteenth century. Along with other collected tales they became popular in the nurseries of the nineteenth-century wealthy middle classes of Europe and America. They were increasingly seen as suitable for children because little moral guidelines had been added to them, but they were already a long way from their origins. These 'folk-fairy' tales began as the pre-literate oral stories of the folk, or common people, and had been told by adults round the fires, in the fields and along the highways. They were not directed at children particularly, but aimed at all the community, so their original themes dealt with the problems, emotions and ambitions of adult men and women. This is why they still have echoes of terrible rage and jealousy (e.g. *Snow White* or *Sleeping Beauty*), early deaths, remarriages and unhappy step-parents and half-siblings (e.g. *Cinderella*), and the horrors of crop failure, starvation and the abandoning of children (e.g. *Jack and the Beanstalk* or *Hansel and Gretel*). All the magic in these old tales can be thought of as a kind of communal wishful thinking and daydreaming, not that different from the plans so many modern folk make for the day when they hope to win the lottery.

There are a number of approaches to explaining the endless appeal of folk-fairy tales and anything goes – from full-blown Freudian analyses (Bettelheim 1976) to Marxist and feminist theories (Zipes 1979). But for the early years educator the 'anything goes' potential of the tales is the clue to their value. In the minds of young children the themes and characters of folk-fairy tales become all-purpose flexible symbols for whatever the child wants them to stand for at any one time. It is a bit like having stories made of Playdough that can be stretched, shaped, pummelled and re-formed as necessary, although they never become shapeless blobs (like Playdough) but spring back to be the tale they always were! This availability and elasticity also applies to the story settings: they are never too specific (a forest, a cottage, a far-off land) and the time is always an unspecified past – long ago or once upon a time. Characters are often known only by their occupations and characteristics (e.g. a brave woodcutter or a wicked queen), or have names that tell us about their appearance and behaviour (e.g. *Goldilocks* or *Cinderella*). Importantly for young children, most of the main characters are small, poor and vulnerable, and survive by a combination of courage and wit, with the help of magical talking animals or superhuman carers who always turn up just at the right time. It is interesting that some of the worst enemies are huge people (giants and ogres), terrible hungry beasts, cruel step-parents and witches, or characters who set the young child/pig/billy-goat mind-blowing riddles to solve. Without being too fanciful ourselves we can see that strange and unpredictable adults may seem like giants and psychoanalytic studies suggest that young children do fear being eaten (adults may say playfully, 'I'm going to gobble you up'). Parents who deny their children things, or become angry with them, are best seen by the temporarily rejected child as not their 'real' parent and a witch can be an angry and unacceptable version of mother (see Anthony Browne's illustrations for *Hansel and Gretel* 1981). As for the riddles and mysteries, life must seem like that for much of the time when you are under 7 years old!

The tales of ordinary folk can be found in all cultures, and they tell of our universal struggles to provide food and survive (e.g. *Bringing the Rain to Kapiti Plain*, Aardema and Vidal 1981), to rear our children and see them happy in adult relationships (e.g. *Mufaro's Beautiful Daughters*, Steptoe 1987), or to cope with our own greed and folly (e.g. *Brother Eagle, Sister Sky*, Jeffers and Chief Seattle 1991).

Myths and legends

Myths and legends are also a long-surviving group of traditional stories and there are some beautifully illustrated and well-written versions being published. Myths and legends are more than the common stories of a pre-literate culture – they are the religious explanations of how the world began, how human beings were created and what kind of relationships existed between them and their gods, and how the human species relates to natural creation. These are huge themes and myths do carry the belief systems of a culture, so that in a multicultural society they are particularly significant. Legends tend to be more focused on outstanding human heroes and heroines, especially those who are great leaders of their people. But legends are not always about kings, queens and emperors – they often tell of rebels who defy gods or kings in order to protect and help common humanity (e.g. Prometheus, Ram and Sita, Robin Hood, Superman).

The references above to superheroes are a reminder of how significant these are in young children's play, drama, drawing and story writing. However, the energetic superhero play of young boys with its apparently violent content and the use of 'weapons' (toy, imaginary and improvised) makes many practitioners and some parents uncomfortable. Current research (Holland 2003; DCSF 2008a) suggests that young boys do play differently from many girls and need very energetic and boisterous role-play opportunities and the chance to work through their high-energy exploratory play. The sensitive support of adults can be crucial in helping boys to extend their imaginary play into more complex scenarios and develop social awareness and respect for others.

It seems that young children do need to try out the feelings of having great power – after all, for much of the time they are powerless and vulnerable while adults exercise control over them (and how often do we attempt to explain our actions and decisions to young children?). Furthermore, legends and myths raise the moral dilemmas and religious questions we all have to answer and early exposure to them in exciting story form should be at the heart of our moral and religious curriculum. The great value of myths and legends in a multicultural society must be the access they give to the core beliefs and traditions of many groups. For young children, opportunities to hear and act out the creation stories of many cultures, or explore their relationships with their gods and the natural world, or share in the stories behind their festivals, may set the tone for a lifetime of openness towards people with different backgrounds and beliefs.

Nursery rhymes

The origins of nursery rhymes are incredibly diverse and often argued about, but the good side to this is that they have no official versions and are open to being altered and adapted by adults and children. Some of the rhymes are ancient and predate the spread of literacy; others are snippets from old song books, political satires, plays and religious writings. In common with most of the traditional literature we use with our young children, nursery rhymes were not originally intended for the family nursery and playroom (with the exception of a few verses – for example, 'Twinkle, twinkle, little star', written by Jane Taylor in 1806 – which are not anonymous and were published for children). The best-known traditional rhymes still have reminders of their origins in ballads, folk songs, church rituals and prayers, drinking songs, street cries, wars, rebellions and romantic lyrics. Generations of children must have picked up these verses as their families sung them and generations of carers must have rocked and comforted restless babies with the catchy little tunes and rhymed verses that were in circulation. The fact that these were the 'pop songs' of whole communities explains their gusto, humour and cruelty, for they reflect a world of rough courtships, whippings and heavy drinking and no amount of Victorian 'cleaning up' has fully disguised this.

An important aspect of the appeal of this material for young children is its wild excesses and cruelties. The children can sing about terrible behaviour, and even enjoy the shock value of doing so, while also feeling some sense of how unacceptable it really is to slit someone's tongue, throw an old man down the stairs or drown a cat in a well. Another dominant theme is, of course, nonsense and the previous chapter suggested that play with language and ideas helps children to understand and manage the realities of their lives. By simply turning things 'on their heads' children can test how they work and how far they can be stretched. The far-fetched jokes and nonsense of nursery rhymes are very similar to young children's own humour and may strengthen children's hold on 'what is what', 'who is who' and 'where is where'. After all, young children soon work out that only complete idiots go to sea in sieves, comb their hair with the leg of a chair and burn their mouths on cold porridge, while even a city child knows that cows do not jump over the moon. The stupidity of so many characters in nursery rhymes must be a great morale booster for children who already know that they would not be as daft as Simple Simon who went whale-fishing in a bucket.

There are many other themes and preoccupations in nursery rhymes, from the difficulties of managing naughty children who go out to play at night, steal pigs and scorch their new clothes to the adult problems of courtship and having too many children. But the most enchanting feature of them is their song-like rhythm and rhyme, and this musical quality ensures that the terrible 'goings-on' are distant and unthreatening, while the words and tunes are highly memorable. Familiarity with the alliteration, rhyme and word play that feature so strongly in traditional nursery rhymes was identified by linguists some decades ago as a crucial factor in young children's early successful reading (Bryant and Bradley 1985; Goswami and Bryant 1990). Research seems to indicate that although some children may have difficulties tuning in to phonological features and wordplay (Goswami 2008), families and practitioners can best prepare children for literacy by nurturing:

- early knowledge of nursery rhymes;
- awareness of rhyme and alliteration;
- the invention of rhymes and alliterative words;
- awareness of the beginning sounds of words;
- awareness of the end sounds of words.

Nursery rhymes are rather like a very special kind of toy that children can take over and play with – sometimes to bounce and dance to, sometimes to muck about with the language, and sometimes to explore ideas about what is forbidden, naughty, frightening or just plain puzzling.

Traditional literature puts children in touch with their cultural past and is a unique example of the rhythms and poetry of spoken language. It also contains symbols that are in tune with the emotional and social concerns and anxieties of young children.

Picture books

The modern picture book is the most exciting and challenging aspect of children's literature and artists, writers and publishers almost fall over themselves to be involved in picture books. The linking of picture books with babies and non-readers has often obscured their literary and educational qualities, but there is no excuse for this misunderstanding now that there are many superb and highly sophisticated picture books available for older children and adults. The fact that picture books have 'grown up', and gone 'up market' is partly due to the new technologies of colour printing and book production, but it is also affected by our increased psychological knowledge of just how complex the skills of reading pictures and combining picture meanings with textual (print) meanings really are.

The apparent simplicity of the picture book is also the reason for its complexity because the very lack, or sparsity, of words means that the reader must work very hard to create the narrative from all the clues provided by the pictures. And pictures can show many things happening at once, so lots of choices and decisions have to be made by picture-book readers of any age. For example, *Rosie's Walk* (Hutchins 1968) teases the reader by telling one very simple story in the text and telling a much more dangerous and comical story in the pictures. The sophisticated artwork in such books as *Where the Wild Things Are* (Sendak 1967) and *The Bear Under the Stairs* (Cooper 1993) contains humour, anarchy and tenderness as well as ambiguity about such matters as what is real, what is imagined and what will happen next. It takes many rereadings to get to grips with all these layers of possibilities and it seems that very young children and adults can find new readings every time they return to the pictures. This understanding that picture books are complex and challenging has led to a huge increase in the academic study of them and much of this work indicates that they have an important part to play in the development of early literacy.

The significance of picture books for literacy may be summarized in the following ways: first, they require that very young children behave like active readers. This means that picture book readers must work out, or theorize, from the title, pictures and words what the plot is likely to be about (wild things, bear under the stairs, peace at last); hunt for the main characters (where is the green parrot, where's Spot); and predict what might happen next (*Each Peach Pear Plum* (Ahlberg and Ahlberg 1977), *Handa's Surprise* (Browne 1994)).

Second, picture books start the literary habit of helping readers to make connections between books and life. We see this as children and toddlers point to objects they recognize in a book, or even go off and bring the object to the book if possible (Miffy's drinking mug, Spot's school bag, an avocado pear). Many picture book authors/illustrators go even further by creating characters who munch real holes in the book (e.g. *The Very Hungry Caterpillar* (Carle 1970)), or play 'peepo' through actual spy-holes in the pages (e.g. *Peepo* (Ahlberg and Ahlberg 1981)), and even tell us that they have accidentally got stuck in the book (*The Little Mouse Trapped in a Book* (Felix 1975)). What all this is doing for babies and early years readers is involving them in a book world so that they bring their experiences to it, but also teaching them how to borrow the book's characters and events to add to their own store of explanations for things that happen (Paddington's got red wellies like mine'; 'our cat eats six dinners'; 'the snowman sat in a freezer like ours').

Third, all these experiences with picture books teach most of the basic literary conventions: beginnings and ways in to narrative; plot complications, problems and challenges; the resolving of difficulties; and happy endings. We know this has been effective when young children begin to use these literary devices in their own oral stories and early writing.

Finally, and most obviously, picture books have small and manageable examples of print so that young emerging readers are gradually introduced to the notion that the black marks carry meanings, as do the pictures. Furthermore, small chunks of print (words) can be examined carefully and they gradually become associated with the repeated appearances of favourite characters. As young readers notice individual letters they are often linked with the increasingly familiar letters in their own names, or the names of brothers and sisters ('I begin like Nellie the elephant' [Natalie]). Picture books play a complex and significant part in introducing children to literature and preparing them for literacy.

Information picture books

Many quality picture books for young children have considerable information content that can extend children's current interests and introduce new ones. One case study of a boy's first three years with picture books noted how rich in factual information his favourite books were, inspiring passionate enthusiasms for sharks, whales, dinosaurs, trains, trucks, diggers, stars and space (Whitehead 2002). Many parents and carers find themselves buying and borrowing books about dinosaurs, robots and steam trains in order to keep up with their children's enthusiasm and visiting museums, railway stations and aquaria. Picture books can develop young children's expert knowledge and start a lifetime's habit of using books as one source of information. The fact that picture books can convey information while telling a good story is developmentally appropriate because young children do not make sharp distinctions between 'facts' or 'fictions'. A handful of recently published picture books tackle such demanding information as the nature of gravity, the eating habits of wolves, the system used in lending libraries, the naming of dinosaurs and the behaviour of nocturnal mammals!

Picture books and reading development

- Picture books require very young children to behave like active readers. They must work out from the titles, pictures and words (if there are any!) what the plot is about; they must identify the main characters; they must predict what might happen next.
- Picture books begin to help emergent readers make connections between books and life. Babies and toddlers point to objects they recognize in books; they 'borrow' book characters and events to help them understand the world.
- Picture books teach the basic literary conventions: beginnings, plot complications, resolutions of difficulties and satisfactory endings.
- Picture books have small samples of meaningful print, considerable repetition and bold initial letters and recognizable character names. They also take liberties with text and print and have memorable words like 'BOO' or 'WHAM', or text that explodes or trots up and down stairs!

Supporting young listeners and tellers

Encouraging young children to tell their own stories and listen to the stories we can tell them and read to them is the most significant contribution we can make to ensuring that they become not just efficiently literate, but passionately hooked on books and keen to write. We now know that it is never too soon to begin sharing books with our babies and we can take advantage of the fact that libraries are at last eager to welcome baby and toddler borrowers. Supermarkets are also making big efforts to stock a range of good-quality books for young children in low-cost paperback form. But even if we cannot afford to buy books we probably have wonderful collections of old rhymes, tongue-twisters, songs, and finger and toe rhymes (e.g. This little piggy went to market; Tommy thumb; Ten little squirrels) locked away in our memories. Or, if we really have no remembered folk material from our cultural inheritance to share, we can get help from older people and other community leaders, or community bookshops, social clubs, child welfare clinics and libraries.

This social and community approach to helping our babies and young children begin the journey to literacy is far better than waiting for schools to do it all. In fact, without the active help and involvement of carers and communities, schools cannot succeed in teaching literacy to all our children. There is a great danger in believing that there are easy short cuts to literacy that can be ordered by government and simply carried out by teachers. Literacy is a complex achievement with roots deep in the earliest days of infancy and all carers, families and early years professionals are teachers of literacy as they sing nursery rhymes, rock babies to sleep with old songs, tell stories about their own childhoods, listen to toddlers' tales of monsters under the bed and share picture books.

Summary

Stories are organized ways of telling about events, feelings, ideas, and so on and the organizing device in stories is narrative. Narrative orders events in time, as does human memory, and narrative is also concerned with values, attitudes, choices and judgements. Narratives permeate cultures and communities, as well as individual lives and behaviour. Community narratives are usually about origins, beliefs and moral and social values. The personal stories we tell ourselves about our lives are ways of thinking and ways of coping and they emerge very early in childhood. In schools, important cultural narratives are passed on in the 'subjects' of the curriculum, but the most important narratives of cultures and individual human experience are found in traditional stories and published books. For these reasons, storytelling, books and literature must be at the heart of the early years curriculum. Knowledge of the genres of literature offers helpful guidance to adults on the range and variety of stories they can share with children.

Provision and activities

- *People*   See the suggestions under this heading at the end of Chapter 2.
- *Places*   See the suggestions under this heading at the end of Chapters 1 and 2.
- *Things to do*   All the suggestions under this heading at the end of Chapters 1 and 2 are relevant because literacy and language development go hand in hand.

This chapter has given detailed guidance on how to approach storytelling, but some comments on sharing a book with a baby and some suggestions for books to use with young children follow.

Sharing a book with a baby

Choose moments when the baby is alert and you are not distracted by other people or jobs to do. Make yourself and the baby comfortable (a personal choice this – sitting on the floor, on cushions, on a bed or in a comfy chair) and choose a book that is easy to hold near the baby's focus (probably only a few inches) and reach (touching pages and pictures is to be encouraged). The choice of book should be decided by such matters as your enjoyment of the story or rhyme, your pleasure in singing and rocking with the rhythms of the language, your pleasure in the words (if any), and how much you like the illustrations and are able to make up stories about them. For the baby's sake you must be prepared to repeat the same books many times and start with a small collection, which can become familiar and well loved, before adding new books. Try to keep the baby's books together in a special place, preferably low down and accessible for a toddler once the crawling and walking stages are reached. At first, book sessions with a baby will be brief and depend on how long the baby is focused on the activity, but the opportunity can also be extended by singing and dancing with the baby or playing music.

Some book suggestions

Folk-fairy tales

The Puffin Baby and Toddler Treasury (Viking 1998).
The Tale of the Turnip by Brian Alderson and Fritz Wegner (Walker Books 1999).
Jim and the Beanstalk by Raymond Briggs (Hamish Hamilton/Puffin 1970).
A Dark, Dark Tale by Ruth Brown (Andersen 1981).
The Princess and the Pea by Lauren Child and Polly Borland (Puffin 2005).
The Little Red Hen by Michael Foreman (Andersen 1999).
Flossie and the Fox by Patricia McKissak (Puffin 1986).
The Story of Chicken Licken by Jan Ormerod (Walker Books 1985).
Hansel and Gretel by Jane Ray (Walker Books 1997).
Goldilocks and the Three Bears by Tony Ross (Andersen 1976).
The Three Little Wolves and the Big Bad Pig by Eugene Trivizas (Heinemann 1993).

Myths and legends

The Mousehole Cat by Antonia Barber (Walker Books 1990).
Atticus the Storyteller's 100 Greek Myths by Lucy Coats and Anthony Lewis (Orion 2002).
Creation Stories from Around the World by Ann Pilling (Walker Books 1997).
Mufaro's Beautiful Daughters by John Steptoe (Hodder & Stoughton 1987).

Nursery rhymes and poetry

Bringing the Rain to Kapiti Plain by Verna Aardema (Macmillan 1981).
A Caribbean Dozen by John Agard and Grace Nichols (Walker Books 1994).
Each Peach Pear Plum by Janet and Allan Ahlberg (Picture Lions 1977).
Quentin Blake's Nursery Rhyme Book by Quentin Blake (Cape 1995).
Husherbye by John Burningham (Cape 2000).
The Orchard Book of Funny Poems edited by Wendy Cope (Orchard 1993).
This Little Puffin by Elizabeth Matterson (Puffin 1969).
My Very First Mother Goose by Iona Opie (Walker Books 1996).
We're Going on a Bear Hunt by Michael Rosen and Helen Oxenbury (Walker
  Books 1989).
Mustard, Custard, Grumble Belly and Gravy by Michael Rosen and Quentin
  Blake (Bloomsbury 2006).
The Cat in the Hat by Dr Seuss (Harper Collins 1957).
A Child's Garden of Verses (1885) by Robert Louis Stevenson. Illustrated by
  Michael Foreman (Gollancz 1997).

Picture books

Ten, Nine, Eight by Molly Bang (Puffin 1983).
Clown by Quentin Blake (Cape 1995).
My Brother Sean by Petronella Breinburg (Puffin 1973).
The Bear by Raymond Briggs (Red Fox 1994).
Granpa by John Burningham (Puffin 1984).
Jasper's Beanstalk by Nick Butterworth (Hodder & Stoughton 1992).
The Bear Under the Stairs by Helen Cooper (Picture Corgi 1993).
Pumpkin Soup by Helen Cooper (Doubleday 1998).
Orange Pear Apple Bear by Emily Gravett (Macmillan 2006).
The Odd Egg by Emily Gravett (Macmillan 2008).
Alfie Gets in First by Shirley Hughes (Picture Lions 1981).
Rosie's Walk by Pat Hutchins (Puffin 1968).
One More Sheep by Mij Kelly and Russell Ayto (Hodder 2004).
Two Bears and Joe by Penelope Lively (Viking 1995).
Not Now, Bernard by David McKee (Arrow 1980).
Six Dinner Sid by Inga Moore (Simon & Schuster 1990).
Five Minutes Peace by Jill Murphy (Walker Books 1986).
The Bear in the Cave by Michael Rosen. Illustrated by Adrian Reynolds
  (Bloomsbury 2007).
Where The Wild Things Are by Maurice Sendak (Puffin 1967).
Can't You Sleep Little Bear? by Martin Waddell (Walker Books 1988).
Farmer Duck by Martin Waddell and Helen Oxenbury (Walker Books 1991).

Owl Babies by Martin Waddell and Patrick Benson (Walker 1992).
Blue Rabbit and Friends by Chris Wormell (Red Fox 1999).

Alphabet books

Quentin Blake's ABC by Quentin Blake (Jonathan Cape 1989).
The Amazing Lift-The-Flap ABC by Colin and Jacqui Hawkins (Mathew Price 2006).
What's Inside? The Alphabet Book by Satoshi Kitamura (A&C Black 1985).
Michael Rosen's ABC by Michael Rosen (Macdonald Young Books 1996).
Dr Seuss's ABC by Dr Seuss (Collins 1963).
F-Freezing ABC by Posy Simmonds (Jonathan Cape 1995).

Information Picture Books

Window by Jeannie Baker (Walker 2002).
Ten Seeds by Ruth Brown (Andersen 2001).
Dear Zoo by Rod Campbell (Macmillan 1982).
Ice Bear by Nicola Davies and Gary Blythe (Walker 2005).
Slow Loris by Alexis Deacon (Hutchinson 2002).
Wolves by Emily Gravett (Macmillan 2005).
Egg Drop by Mini Grey (Cape 2002).
Water Witcher by Jan Ormerod (Little Hare 2006).
Harry and the Bucketful of Dinosaurs by Ian Whybrow and Adrian Reynolds (David & Charles 1999).
Harry and the Dinosaurs go to School by Ian Whybrow and Adrian Reynolds (David & Charles 2006).

Further reading

Butler, D. (1979) *Cushla and Her Books*. Sevenoaks: Hodder & Stoughton.
Engel, S. (1995) *The Stories Children Tell: Making Sense of the Narratives of Childhood*. New York: W.H. Freeman.
Fox, C. (1993) *At the Very Edge of the Forest: The Influence of Literature on Storytelling by Children*. London: Cassell.
Gamble, N. and Yates, S. (2007) *Exploring Children's Literature: Teaching the Language and Reading of Fiction*, 2nd edn. London: Paul Chapman.
Lewis, D. (2001) *Reading Contemporary Picturebooks: Picturing Text*. London: Routledge.
Whitehead, M.R. (2002) Dylan's routes to literacy: the first three years with picture books, *Journal of Early Childhood Literacy*, 2(3): 269–89.

4

Emerging literacy

As I sounded the words 'cheep 'cheep' in one story for example Cecilia (3–4) remarked, that's like 'cheese' and as the word 'supper' in the story of *John Brown, Rose and the Midnight Cat* was read she observed 'That's like shopping 'cos it's got two 'p's. A further example revealed the actual word scanning process in operation even though it was a short word. Cecilia (3–3) identified the word 'zoo' and remarked 'That's got two "o"s and a zebra'.

(Payton 1984: 80)

This chapter focuses on:

- representation, mark-making and early writing;
- finding out about print;
- early writing – strategies and milestones;
- reading for meaning;
- close encounters with words and sounds.

Three-year-old Cecilia's confident and highly personal ability to recognize the sounds and letters of words in her favourite books indicates that literacy begins early and is rooted in the kinds of experience with people, languages and print described in the previous three chapters. In just over three years a child may move from her first gasping cries at birth to Cecilia's brilliant word recognition and analysis of 'two "o"s and a zebra'. This remarkable journey begins with the baby's desire to communicate, as outlined in Chapter 1, and is all about making and sharing meanings with carers and others. The possibilities of playing with language, sounds and meanings add some interesting features to early language learning (see Chapter 2) and the child's literacy journey gets more exciting as the possibilities of stories and narrative reveal a new landscape (see Chapter 3). So, many more ways of making sense of our experiences are available in stories and books, including opportunities for exploring personal identity and our links with family groups and cultures. Stories also fortify us – adults as much as children – against anxiety, loss and the many disasters and mishaps of life. The remarkable way in which literacy, or the writing system of a culture, continues and expands these possibilities and accelerates the wonderful start many young children have made as communicators, meaning-makers, linguists and storytellers will be the subject of this chapter.

Representation

Literacy certainly gets started long before most parents and carers recognize it and the widely accepted academic view is that literacy begins with the thinking processes and activities known broadly as *representation*. This is a rather daunting theory but we can turn to Cecilia for a little help and guidance as we explore it. In the passage quoted above she describes the letter 'z' in 'zoo' as 'zebra', and we can assume that her most vivid and frequent encounters with the letter 'z' have been as the initial letter of 'zebra'. Many young children are excited and attracted by pictures (in books and on television) of the dramatically black-and-white striped horse-like zebra, often accompanied by its word label, and for English speakers and readers the rarely occurring initial letter 'z' is a highly memorable letter shape. For Cecilia, 'zebra' actually represents 'z' – it is a visual, emotional and written symbol that packs a special kind of punch for her whenever she meets it. Symbols work like this for all of us – they are a focus for our feelings and stand for, or represent, whole ranges of emotions, thoughts, experiences and cultural traditions (just think how often British children see zebras in alphabet books and friezes, and in animal and zoo books). Such symbolic representations actually help us to think, whatever our age, because they provide ready-made summaries of complicated events and experiences. Children also make marks and drawings that are their personal symbolic representations or summaries at a very early age and families and early childhood settings often display these pictures of 'mum', 'a tree', 'a lorry', and so on. Representations help children and adults to hold on to, or recall, things and people in their absence (e.g. a zebra seen previously in a picture alphabet book), and to make new connections between similar images, objects, events and marks (e.g. this word 'zoo' starts like my special favourite 'zebra').

Representations have been described as a huge family of activities (Matthews 2003) and also include such important forms of early childhood thinking and action as talk, play, stories, mime, dance, model-making and building, mark-making, painting, drawing and writing. Young children participate in all these activities and use them as ways of representing or thinking through their experiences of – and present knowledge about people, emotions, life and the entire universe! Many observations of children's representational thinking can be found in the previous chapters; for example, the play repertoire of the little girl on the tube train. Now we have to add to this family of representational thinking activities the processes of early writing and reading, but a word of warning about the 'special' nature of literacy may be useful at this point.

Warning!

Although the process of representational thinking (including early mark-making) may be a natural and distinctive feature of our species (like verbal language), literacy is a latecomer in human history and is a cultural invention of human groups. Some highly complex societies in the past did not evolve writing systems and it is a fairly modern idea to expect all the individuals in a society to read and write competently. The universal ability to read and write is a measure of social, educational and economic progress in most contemporary cultures, while for individuals being literate makes all the difference to their chances of social acceptability, worthwhile employment, extended educational opportunities and material success. These hugely important issues explain not just the power of literacy but the pain and the pressure it puts on young children and their families and communities. Knowing the terrible handicaps of illiteracy in our society and desperate to see our own children reading and writing we may, with the best of intentions, adopt approaches and practices that make reading and writing narrow and pointless. This will undermine our children's true literacy interests and strategies. However, this is not a 'lay off teaching' warning, but a 'trust and observe young learners so that you know what help and information to give' plea, and it underpins the entire philosophy of this book.

The discussion of children's literacy development that follows will begin with 'writing' because, contrary to many assumptions, children's early writing often starts long before reading, although looking at books and listening to stories feed into early writing attempts and accelerate the development of early understanding of the alphabet and spelling.

Making marks

Very young children make marks as they smear their spilt food across a table or wall, drag their fingers through pools of liquid, use a lipstick on a mirror, scribble over the print in books and magazines, or even get to grips with the paper, paint, pens and crayons adults prefer them to use. There is also growing evidence that very young children who have access to computer word-processing and paint programs make similar marks and drawings (Kent 1997). It is all too easy to dismiss these marks as 'scribbles' and 'mess' and of no significance, yet a moment's thought should convince us that exciting things are happening. For a start, these young children are making their mark in the world (Figure 4.1) and this is a

Figure 4.1 Making a mark in the world.

metaphor we frequently use to praise someone's achievements, although it originates in the days when illiterate adults could only sign documents by 'making their mark' (usually a cross). More importantly, children's early mark-making activities have three major characteristics that are usually associated with literacy: creativity, communication and some degree of permanence.

Creativity

The idea that early marks are creative is not an exaggeration because even a sticky chocolate smear on a wall or tablecloth is new in the world, it is the trace of an action and evidence of the existence of the child who made the mark. These first marks may begin as 'accidents' but they stay long enough to be noticed, commented and even repeated on other occasions and with other tools (because chocolate on walls does not always get the praise that early mark-making deserves!). A long process of creative mark-making is triggered by these first happy accidents with food, dribbles, damp surfaces and the more conventional materials used for writing in homes and care settings. Researchers suggest that first mark-making is triggered by an inner developmental programme (Matthews 2003), rather like verbal language and walking, and that these early marks are representations of movement, space, shape and emotions. In simple terms, very young children are making a movement with a marker for the pleasurable physical sensations it gives, or exploring shape and space as they experience them, and also working through varied feelings and emotional responses. If all these things occur while markers and surfaces of some kind are to hand then a permanent representation (or mark/picture) of the experience is made. Is this so very different from all the art forms that human groups have developed over the centuries?

Communication

The marks made by young children certainly communicate the fact that the young mark-makers exist, but children soon begin to use their own marks as 'signs' that carry messages. So they start to give their marks names or labels – for example, 'a lorry', 'a worm' – in a similar fashion to the way older children and adults 'recognize' the shapes of faces and animals in cloud formations. As children's marks become more like drawings – or representations of generally recognizable objects – the young artists will explain them with story-like captions: 'All the people in the house' (Payton 1984: 38). This is a very common example of children making sense of experience and using their own representations as a powerful kind of thinking and communication. So strong is young children's drive to understand all kinds of representation and make sense of them that they will even 'humanize' geometrical shapes (see Figure 4.2). This drawing is by a 4-year-old (4 years 3 months) Chinese girl in a London primary school nursery class who was given some plastic logi-blocks to draw round, but then found her own way of making human sense of the task.

Figure 4.2 A child has made a drawing from the outlines of plastic geometric shapes.

Permanence

Marks, like writing and print, are permanent in that they exist long enough for us to think about them and/or save them for others to see and share.

Marks and writing can be destroyed and there is certainly a place in all good literacy learning and teaching for waste-paper bins, recycle bins and shredders, but writing and early marks can also be corrected, changed and improved. Very young children's mark-making changes as it is influenced by the print they encounter in their immediate environments and by the enthusiasm of adults who recognize and praise these attempts at writing. Even the scribble patterns of young children begin to look like the flowing lines of 'real writing' and collections of apparently random marks – as well as drawings and paintings – start to include recognizable letters and numerals.

The desire to communicate and create permanent messages leads many young children to put marks on family shopping lists, answer pads, notes and letters, or write their own versions of their names on books, magazines, drawings and scraps of paper. These developments are at the heart of literacy because the young communicators are 'joining the literacy club' (Smith 1988) of their culture by creating messages ('"Mummy, this says someone's crying, someone's singing, someone's playing Lord Kumba Ya" (Cecilia 3–8)' (Payton 1984: 45)) and receiving the messages of others ('"Where it say 'toot'?" (Cecilia 3–3)' (Payton 1984: 68)). During these early stages in the literacy process children already experience something of the organizing power and emotional impact of the written system. They make lists and inventories of names and logos they know (people, pets, shops, foods or even storybook characters – see Figure 4.3), or use their names as markers of ownership on books, toys and doors, or as signs of love and affection on scraps of paper given as presents to special friends and carers. But at this point the nature of mark-making is changing as young children begin to investigate print closely and find out about its relationships to the sounds of their languages.

Writing sounds

It is helpful to think of young children's early writing as a response to an exciting literacy problem: how do you break into the system that encodes (puts into written/graphic symbols) the sounds and meanings of spoken language so that you can be a full member of 'the literacy club'? The first step in tackling this problem is to ask the right questions and get help from those 'in the know'. The sooner this happens the better, as the studies of sharing books with babies are indicating, and it is clear that young children find little difficulty in asking the right questions if certain optimum conditions are maintained. The nature and pacing of the help given by

Figure 4.3 The names of storybook characters.

carers and educators requires sensitivity and insight of the sort that comes from close and caring involvement with young children and a desire to learn more about them.

Asking the right questions about print

The right questions can be summarized as:

- What does that say?
- How do you write . . . ?

How often have we all half-heard these questions from a young child and not realized how significant they are for literacy development? With these two broad questions about print, young children are hypothesizing or creating theories about how the entire system works. The answers we give must be as prompt and as well-tuned as possible to the child's requirements and as simply honest and true as we can make them. These major questions about literacy are huge achievements in themselves and reflect some very sophisticated thinking by young children about the nature of communication, spoken language, print and representing sounds by grouping graphic signs in regular patterns. These are complex ideas for all of us and they cannot readily be simplified but we do not have to launch into complicated explanations in response to our children's literacy questions. We just have to behave like enthusiastic and helpful writers and readers ourselves and tell our children what the print 'says' and show them how to write their own words and messages.

For example, during meals or at the shops we can read the words and the instructions on the packets and wrappers of familiar foods: 'That word is "Sugarpops", see the "S" it starts with? What else do you like to eat that starts with "S"? ... Smarties – that's right! Shall we write Smarties on our shopping list for this afternoon?'

Of course this is a slightly exaggerated example and not all these questions need to be asked at any one time, but it does illustrate the opportunities for investigating and learning about literacy in the homeliest of situations.

Optimum conditions

The responses we make to children's questions about print will demonstrate some of the ways in which sounds are written, but even to get to first base in literacy does require some optimum conditions. Clearly children cannot ask the right questions about print if they do not encounter enough of it to rouse their curiosity, nor will they risk the questions and make 'good guesses' if the whole business appears to be threatening and creates anxiety. However, we can create the optimum literacy conditions for young children in remarkably simple ways and the following slogans may be helpful indicators:

Optimum literacy conditions

- Print should be for real.
- Print should be for pleasure.
- Print should be for proper investigation.

Print for real

Print for real is no problem in the contemporary world that swamps us with printed matter, and although swamping young children is not intended here, the everyday kind of print we find in our homes, streets, shops and clubs, and on our clothes, televisions and computers is particularly useful. It is genuine print about real things that matter to people and it is easily found, played with and thrown away when it gets tatty. It is often associated with good motivating experiences such as: visits to fast-food restaurants; trips on buses and trains; gifts on special occasions; letters from relatives; visits to places of worship; pretending to be a grown-up filling in forms in the bank or post office; and favourite cereals and yoghurts collected from the supermarket shelf. All you need is bags of everyday print and, if possible, access to a QWERTY keyboard or computer word-processing program (see Kent 1997). There is no necessity to buy special early writing and reading exercise books or expensive software that promises to teach 'pre-school children' all about the alphabet, phonics and spelling. These materials will not allow the children to ask their own questions about print and invent their own experimental systems for writing, and they may instil a belief that there is only one right answer to every question and wrong answers must be avoided.

Print for pleasure

Print should be for pleasure and we must provide young children with ample opportunities to play and muck about with the system – hence the importance of collecting and using cheap and meaningful materials. The atmosphere in which we play at being readers and writers with our children must also be relaxed and open-ended so that they feel able to take risks and exploit words, sounds and graphic symbols (see Featherstone 2006). Chapter 2 is of direct relevance here and it is at this point that we need to be sure that our children encounter songs, chants, rhymes, tongue-twisters, poetry and rhythmic dances and games every day.

Print for investigation

Print should be available for close investigation because children learn in ways that are very like the behaviour of serious scientists: they observe closely, hypothesize or tell a possible story about what they have noticed, and then try out this theory on the material or event that has interested them. If this does not give an acceptable explanation they try to change the parts of their theory that appear to be adrift. An example of this approach to spoken language and word meanings was given in Chapter 2 when my grandson Daniel had to revise his hypothesis about my use of the word 'ornamental' in referring to some ducks. When it comes to investigating print a young child may see the name of a supermarket chain that starts with 'S' and announce 'That says my name – Sanjay'. The child does not believe that he is called 'Sainsbury' but he is aware of the significance of initial letters and the sound that is common to the beginning of his name and that of the grocery store. My granddaughter developed an early fascination with initial letters and created her own alphabets as well as using initial letters to label the figures in her many drawings of kings, queens, princesses and beautiful ladies (see Figure 4.4). Here we have evidence of an early start to finding out about English spelling patterns by a 4-year-old bilingual child. Her interest was stimulated by wide exposure to at least three languages and lots of different alphabets – in books, on posters and friezes – and by having fun making lists of people, places, foods, animals, and so on that start with the same sounds.

Figure 4.4 Initial letters on drawings by a 4-year-old.

Young writers' strategies

Young children have their own strategies for finding out more about how to write sounds and when these are supported by caring and knowledgeable adults, they take the children a long way towards understanding the system. I have written about these strategies before (Whitehead 2007) and will only outline them briefly here.

- Asking direct questions.
- Watching other people writing.
- Using and writing their own names.
- Exploiting any knowledge about writing.
- Using alphabets and sounds.

Asking questions

Children ask us directly about what print means and how to write it.

Watching others

Children watch other people writing and try to do it themselves, especially when their 'models' are loved and admired. So, they do a shopping list alongside mum, even imitating her sighs, pencil-sucking and the crossing out of items.

Using names

Children's names are full of significance as signs that they exist and have a place in the world, but they are also a very familiar example of a set of sound and symbol combinations that give some clues about how the system works. This means not just initial letters but terminal (end) patterns like 'er' or 'ia' and combinations such as 'ch' and 'st'.

Exploiting knowledge about writing

Even if they only know their own name, or a few letters of it, children will use this ingeniously to create a message. For example, my 3-year-old granddaughter would write letters to me consisting of her name at the top of the paper and the rest of the sheet filled with rows of kisses and letter-like marks. Another child wrote to tell me it was her fourth birthday by filling a page with her name repeated in neat rows and putting a row of 4s (often seen on birthday cakes and cards in her nursery centre) at the bottom of the sheet. These children were using what written signs they did know and having a pretend go at the unknown bits, but they were definitely communicating important human messages (Figure 4.5).

Figure 4.5 Communicating important messages.

Using alphabets and sounds

Young children delight in alphabets and soon recognize initial letters and their sounds; this ties in with their delight in playing with language sounds, rhymes and nonsense. This can lead to the gradual realization that the continuous stream of spoken language must be broken down into separate words and groups of sounds. Many children use the names of letters to create a semi-phonetic code for writing: RUDF = are you deaf? (Bissex 1980: 3). Or they write only the easily heard consonants: TBL = table, NMBR = number.

Some milestones in early writing

There are patterns to young children's development as writers and we need to be sensitive to these and be able to keep observations and records of the milestones. This is particularly important because these developmental processes of literacy are not always valued by conventional approaches to teaching children to write, which concentrate on copying and practising letter formation. However, some valuable guidelines do exist. For instance, the remarkable provision and philosophy in the Reggio Emilia kindergartens of Italy where children are enabled to move from 'gifts of communication' – exchanging objects, messages, words and skills via loans and borrowings – to written messages and love letters, because every child has a personal mailbox (Reggio Emilia 1996; Thornton and Brunton 2007). A British approach to assessing young children's writing (Gorman and Brooks 1996) provides a useful outline of stages to look for, beginning with 'drawing and sign writing' and moving through 'letter-like forms', 'copied letters', 'child's name and strings of letters', 'words', 'sentences' and 'text'. (And ending with 'a bit of theory' for parents and teachers.)

The milestones that follow are based on my own research over a number of years in several London nursery schools and classes and may help you to notice and record the writing development of the young children in your care. They will also help you to understand the achievements of the young children in the case studies in the next chapter.

Milestones in early writing

- Scribble.
- Isolated letters and numerals.
- Lists and inventories.
- Own name.
- Words and pictures.
- Phonological awareness and spelling.

Scribble

This is an important breakthrough as it indicates the child's awareness that 'writing' is not the same as pictures and drawing. Scribble is spiky and often in lines (linear) and even written with the speed and flourish of 'real' writers. (We may need to be wary when we use the word 'scribble' to describe children's writing because many adults use the word to indicate meaningless rubbish!)

Isolated letters and numerals

Both conventional and invented letters and numerals appear in ones, twos or more, scattered among drawings, paintings and lines of scribble. This is evidence of the impact of the conventional written systems children are exposed to in their homes, group settings and communities, and children's growing interest in them.

Lists and inventories

These appear as well-organized listings in horizontal and vertical lines of individual conventional letters and numerals, and invented letter-like forms. A later development will sometimes appear as standard lists of names (friends, family, food, storybook and television characters). These seem to be personal checklists of what the child knows and can write unaided, and also enable the child to create satisfying chunks of text. Later lists may be a way of thinking about and organizing information.

Own name

As discussed above, personal names give children clues about how written language represents the sound system of the spoken language and they are immensely important as badges of identity and ownership. Children can discover written conventions like double consonants (Dennis), alternative spellings and variants (Ann, Anne, Anna) and different languages (Jamila, Yvette, Sian). Children are often very determined to 'get it right' when writing their own names and will self-correct and persevere at the task for long periods. The first isolated letters we find in children's drawings and mark-making are often those from their own names.

Words and pictures

An exciting early development in young children's literacy is the occurrence of pictures accompanied by written captions. These may appear as lines of scribble, collections (strings) of conventional letters, 'words' labelling figures and objects in the drawing, and readable semi-phonetic bits of text. The importance of this milestone is that it once again indicates an understanding of the differences between drawing and writing, but it is also a very significant indicator of the power and influence of books on the child's thinking. The child is beginning to investigate a striking feature of literate and bookish cultures; that is, that pictures and words together tell stories and complement each other.

Phonological awareness and spelling

This is the point at which many children find the courage to trust what they hear and have a go at representing it using letters and groups of letters

Figure 4.6 Martha uses her knowledge of phonics to write.

whose 'sounds' they know. The resulting invented spellings tell us what children understand about written and spoken language and what they are trying to work out next (Figure 4.6). In order to break into conventional spelling young children have to take risks and this means that they must have a strong desire to communicate and be confident that the readers of their communications will respond to the messages appropriately. Some of the most delightful examples of this kind of writing are private notes, letters and complaints: 'I HIVANT HAD A TR IN PAD' (I haven't had a turn in Playdough) (Newkirk 1984: 341). Clearly the problem of democratic and fair access to the Playdough must be sorted out and this 4-year-old should be praised for her excellent grasp of the sounds of American English and their alphabetic representation, before she is encouraged to look at some of the complex patterns of standardized spelling.

Finally, it is important to remember that these are just some milestones that I have noticed and found interesting. They are not rigid stages through which all children should pass and many children do miss out many of them, or pass through them rapidly or when we are not looking. Other people's milestones are only useful if they encourage you to start collecting your own examples of children's marks, drawings and writing, and begin mapping out milestones for the children you know, care for and educate.

Reading for meaning

Many settings are too concerned that children can recognize certain words, so that 'barking at print' becomes the core of the 'hearing children read' session. What adults *should* be encouraging is reading for meaning. This begins with all the important story and narrative activities described in the previous chapter and it is clearly the most important reason for sharing books with babies. In fact, reading for meaning is the foundation of all literacy and any definition of 'reading' that does not have the communication of meaning at its centre is nonsensical. Reading without gaining, or at least searching for, meaning is just performing tricks with print and no more significant than a parrot's mimicry of words. Meaningful reading starts with *shared approaches* in which children and adults are partners; it involves learning to *ask questions of texts* (print and pictures); and it requires that the beginner reader is able to *predict likely outcomes*.

Reading for meaning

- Shared approaches and reading partners
- Asking questions of the text
- Predicting likely outcomes

Shared approaches

Early reading is most successful when children and adults share the pleasures of looking at books, reading them together and talking about them on many occasions. These literary experiences are created by adult–child literacy partnerships in which the older and wiser partner starts by taking on a great deal of the reading and at first leads the discussion about what the text is about. However, this should never leave the child with nothing to do as even a very young child can be helped to focus on the book, point at a picture, bounce up and down to the repeated and rhythmic language patterns or repeat crucial names and phrases from the text (see Chapter 3). Older and more experienced infant readers will know favourite books word for word, be able to read along with the adult, and be able to take over the reading of favourite passages and repeated rhymes and phrases. If wordless picture books or books with very few words are shared, the child can be encouraged to take on much greater responsibility for creating a narrative that is guided by the pictures.

It is worth emphasizing at this point that children who know the words or story of a book 'off by heart' or who use the pictures as cues to recreate the narrative line are doing something that is very skilled and essential to competent reading when they start going it alone. If young children know the words of a book from memory, they actually have a pattern or model of the story in their heads, which they can then match to the pages of the book (the text). Any mismatches that occur as they try to read and then find that they 'run out of' words or pages, or have 'too many left over', will actually help them to focus more closely on the text and on the appearance and patterns of groups of words and individual words. Similarly, the 'reading' of pictures is a sophisticated skill and one at which young children born and brought up with television, video and computer icons soon excel. Such an apparently obvious matter as recognizing similar images of a main character on page after page is a sophisticated literary convention that is gradually understood by young children as they investigate whether there are lots of Little Bears, or just the same Little Bear who cannot get to sleep. An artist's use of horizontal lines, flying clothes and bending trees and grass to indicate running and speed are not 'natural', they are artistic conventions and must be learnt by lots of book sharing and discussions about passages like this: *'Jemima Puddle-Duck was not much in the habit of flying. She ran downhill a few yards flapping her shawl, and then she jumped off into the air'* (Potter [1908] 1989: 163).

Shared partnerships with books bring another bonus: they help children to literally see and hear print being brought to life by a familiar voice. The child can watch the text, hear the words and identify the meanings partly because the human voice can express so much meaning. This is a very important reading lesson for young children who are sitting close to caring adults, seeing the print symbols and hearing the related sounds, whether of wonderful nonsense words like 'Rumpeta, Rumpeta' from *The Elephant and the Bad Baby* (Vipont and Briggs 1969), familiar phrases such as 'Not now, Bernard' (McKee 1980) or a long list of dinosaur names (Whybrow and Reynolds 1999).

Questioning the text

Successful readers learn to ask questions of any text they meet in order to search out its meanings and, just as importantly, its relevance for them. We all scan reading matter in this way – from personal letters and public notices to novels, poems and newspaper stories. Furthermore, successful readers bring their own questions to a text and this is particularly obvious when the text is a reference book or a handbook for some new equipment (How do you reset the clock in this car? Will the microwave defrost a cream cake? Where is Patagonia?). But good readers also bring their own 'life and death' questions to the reading of novels, biographies, history, poetry and even television and radio 'soaps'.

Young children make a very early start on these big questions about the human condition and they are always wanting to know 'who loves me?', 'why do some children not like me?' and 'why do people go away?'. Stories, books, plays and television and radio 'soaps' give children (and adults) the chance to verbalize these difficult questions safely by focusing them on fictional characters and imaginary situations. All that is required for the young child to do this is a reading partner who encourages careful examination of pictures and print, rereads texts many times and creates opportunities for lots of talk about favourite stories, pictures and characters.

The research literature is full of examples of very young readers who are concerned about motives – 'She's nice ain't she? [referring to the beautiful, but wicked, queen in Snow White]' (Payton 1984: 56); emotions – 'Cushla solicitously kissed his howling little face at every reading . . . Her identification with Sean was complete' (Butler 1979: 50); and the unstated aspects of story plots 'Did Rosie know that the fox was following her?' (Hutchins 1968).

Predicting likely outcomes

It is a short step from asking questions of texts to making predictions about what is likely to happen and this is one of the crucial skills for the experienced reader as well as for the young beginner. The ability fluent readers have to pick up meaning at great speed and process lengthy and complex texts without losing their way is rooted in their fast and ever-changing predictions about texts at several levels, including overall meaning, individual word meanings, instant word recognition, letter–sound combinations, print conventions and cultural expectations to name a few! This may be complex but it has to start somewhere and very early encounters between books, babies and adults seem once again to be at the heart of literacy.

Many modern picture books make it particularly easy and enjoyable to predict the outcomes of a situation and talk about life and relationships. One very striking example is the interruption of the printed story line by a series of full page pictures without captions in the middle of *Where the Wild Things Are* (Sendak 1967). This picture sequence occurs at the main pivot of the narrative, a kind of big decision time for Max – will he stay as king of the Wild Things or return home? Young readers are in effect required to participate actively in making this difficult decision as they are drawn into pages of wild rumpus through dream-like jungles with smiling monsters who are remarkably obedient to a small boy in a sleep-suit and a gold crown.

Many picture books use large picture spreads to draw the young reader into thinking about and predicting appropriate moves for fictional characters. Even an Old English Sheepdog can raise some of the most difficult emotional issues in *John Brown, Rose and the Midnight Cat* (Wagner and Brooks 1977) when he is depicted thinking about his jealous reaction to a stray cat. Over several pages of stunning artwork the reader must agonize with this tormented creature and debate the pros and cons of love, loneliness, old age, jealousy and forgiveness.

All this may seem to be strong stuff for small children but books intended for them are as rich in hilarious decisions – will anyone ever buy a dog called '*Arthur*' (Graham and Gynell 1984) who is trying to look like any animal pet except a dog? – as they are in narrow escapes from disasters like locking yourself inside the house, as in *Alfie Gets in First* (Hutchins 1981). It seems that young readers can manage all these challenging predictions if they have a reading partner who helps them to scan pictures closely by talking about them and focusing their attention on certain details: 'Where is Alfie going now? What is he carrying?'; 'What is John Brown thinking about?'; 'Would *you* like to stay with the Wild Things?'. Similar queries can be voiced as we discuss the plot of a favourite book and speculate about what will be left in Handa's basket (Browne 1994), or what Slow Loris (Deacon 2002) gets up to in the night.

Of course this must all be done gently, over time and with many enthusiastic rereadings, but what these features of reading for meaning in the early years do is help children to become active readers. The absolutely essential reading lesson we are sharing with young children at this stage is that reading is an active, searching, thinking, meaning-making and hugely enjoyable experience.

Close encounters with words

Cecilia Payton was looking closely at print before she was three and other babies have been fascinated by the print on calendars and the bold graphics of Dick Bruna's *Miffy* books (Butler 1979). Modern research is still full of observations of young children who learn to love print as much as pictures and understand that it carries messages (Hall 1987; Scrivens 1995; Miller 1996; Campbell 1999). This should give us the confidence to try and stimulate our children's close encounters with print by developing some enjoyable strategies for sharing books and reading print of all kinds. Three helpful strategies for focusing closely on words with a young child are: behaving like *word detectives*, lots of *alphabet play* and noticing and playing with *similar sounds*.

Close encounters with words and sounds

- Behaving like word detectives
- Playing with alphabets
- Playing and experimenting with sounds

Word detectives

Adult encouragement of an investigative and playful approach to close encounters with words helps young children to be active word detectives as they scan print. The aim is to support children so that they develop problem-solving attitudes to all aspects of literacy, search for clues to word identity and meaning and notice regular letter and sound patterns that can be predicted. As children grow in confidence and experience, they are able to bring all their earlier literacy and life experiences to bear on words and texts, but in the early days they need to borrow the experience and skill of an older reading partner. In close one-to-one or small-group book-sharing situations very young children can be shown important words such as characters' names (these often appear in the titles of books and are printed boldly on book covers), place names and authors' and illustrators' names. They can also be shown those powerful words in a text that carry emotional information such as 'love', 'angry', 'kiss', 'happy' and 'cry'. Sometimes special graphic effects are used for these words and others, like 'crash', 'ouch', 'buzz' and 'no' – just like the print effects in comics ('boom', 'splat', 'pow'). All these ways of drawing attention to print and the conventions of spelling develop alphabetic and phonological awareness in exciting and meaningful ways. Furthermore, repeated words that carry lots of meaning and emotional power can soon be recognized by very young readers and they can first join in with saying them and then be encouraged to say them alone while the adult reader stays silent. This applies as much to road names, advertising hoardings and notices in the supermarket as to favourite books. It is a bit like the practice of leaving gaps in early conversations with babies so that they can slot in their gurgles and word approximations.

Alphabet play

Children do need to develop alphabetic awareness so that they can recognize letters of the alphabet, know their names and make a start on as-
sociating them with some of their commoner sounds. We must not be too
rigid about the sounds individual letters make as these vary in English
and are greatly changed by the letters they are grouped with in words and
by certain historical aspects of the development of standardized English
spellings. We must always refer to the sounds of individual letters or letter
strings in meaningful and enjoyable words, texts and stories.

There are lots of opportunities for alphabet play in traditional songs and
rhymes: A was an archer who shot at a frog; Great A, little a, Bouncing
B, The cat's in the cupboard and she can't see me; Pat-cake, pat-a-cake,
baker's man. Or in the nonsense alphabets of Edward Lear (R was a rabbit
Who had a bad habit Of eating the flowers In gardens and bowers), and
the beautiful modern alphabet books, posters and friezes widely available
in shops, libraries and early years settings.

Play with alphabets, common letter sounds and alphabetic order can
be encouraged if children make their own lists of 'things that begin with
A', and so on and move on to building up their own alphabets of things,
people, places and experiences that matter to them. Of course these activities should also involve lots of drawing, cutting and sticking, or using a
computer or typewriter keyboard – as the children see fit, and depending
on resources. Lots of opportunities to look at and play with address books,
telephone directories, A to Z street directories, first dictionaries and word
books can stimulate interest in alphabets and give young children useful
insights into the ways in which letters – singly and in groups – represent
the sounds of the language (see Featherstone 2006).

Similar sounds

Developing young children's sensitivity to the sounds of language – the
same, the similar, the near-echoes and all sorts of variations – can best
be done by surrounding them with poetry, rhyme and verse. From this
jumping-off point we can begin to alert them in their close encounters
with words to the fact that similar sounds will show up as similar spelling
patterns. Of course we would be unwise to put it to them as baldly as that –
we need to play the word detectives game so that they see words which
start with the same letters and hear how similar they sound. This is of
course the poetic device of alliteration and also relates to young children's
interest in initial letters. Sensitivity to initial letters in words comes early
and can often be increased by learning alliterative tongue-twisters and

traditional nursery rhymes (e.g. Davy Davy Dumpling, Boil him in a pot), or noticing some advertising slogans. The same and similar endings of words are soon heard by children who have a rich store of songs and poetry to draw on, because this is the aspect of language sound that we call rhyme. When looking at print with children we can point out the rhymes and draw attention to the fact that words have endings as well as beginnings:

> Dance to your daddy,
> My little babby,
> Dance to your daddy,
> My little lamb.

Once children are enjoying the fact that they can both hear, see and make up their own alliteration and rhymes, it will be a pleasure to look at and talk about the many regular letter strings or combinations that occur in various positions in words. Sometimes these strings will be familiar end rhymes as in 'sing' and 'king', or digraphs like 'ch', 'th' and 'sh', or the double vowel patterns 'ee', 'ea', 'ou', 'oo', and so on.

There is a worrying aspect to this discussion of close encounters with words! In practice it can degenerate into the most pointless and unenjoyable 'phonics' work that is neither accurate in its insights about phonology, nor focused on stimulating children's love of language and books. Most of my examples have come from nursery rhymes and other traditional sources and this is because early encounters with words should be pleasurable, playful and permeating the child's day (please note the alliteration!). Despite the current claims and statutory requirements for early reading teaching in England, the facts are that literacy should *not* be confined to set times and lessons but must be a joyful 24-hour commitment. Furthermore, too formal an approach to literacy in the early years is a recipe for disaster. Professional educators and carers have a responsibility to educate themselves about phonic facts and share this knowledge with parents, other early years professionals and the wider community. A confident understanding of the terms that are frequently used is a good start:

Phonics facts

- *Phonics* is a method for teaching reading that focuses on the relationship between sounds (phonemes) and letters (graphemes). A phoneme is the smallest unit of sound in a language but not necessarily a single letter; for example, 'ee' in 'bee' is a phoneme. Linguists identify approximately 44 phonemes in English.

- *Synthetic phonics* is the so-called 'new' approach required in the reading curricululm in England, but it is also the oldest and most traditional of phonic methods. It claims that simple decoding is all that is required in early reading and teaches the sounds of individual letters and the 44 phonemes of English. Children are taught to sound out the letters in words in sequence and then 'blend' them together. In practice, this means that they must somehow turn 'mer'-'a'-'ter' into 'mat' and risk failing dismally when they get to complex word patterns in a simple text, such as 'said', 'the', 'any'.

- *Analytic phonics* draws on the findings of modern linguistic research and children are taught to look at segments of words and at the frequent patterns in sounds and words. This approach starts by focusing on the beginning, or initial, sounds of words, called 'onset', and the end phonemes called 'rimes'. This can be done by encouraging lots of enjoyable play with the alphabet and the sounds of letters (alphabetic awareness) and children can be helped to enjoy the alliteration of same initial sounds in tongue-twisters and the same, or similar, end rimes found in words that rhyme in songs, poetry and verse (phonological awareness).

Even these very simplified definitions indicate that using phonics in the initial teaching of reading is not going to be a simple and unproblematic strategy for all children and all teachers. Recent professional experience and academic research, much of it from the USA, is highly ambiguous about the advantage of one kind of phonics over another (Meyer 2002; Altwerger 2005). It is more likely that different aspects of phonics are effective at different stages in young children's literacy development. Furthermore, we all get better at using a range of phonic strategies once we are able to read! There is no research support for the notion that every phoneme and every possible spelling 'rule' for English (more than 166, plus many exceptions!) must be taught systematically to every child (Dombey 2006).

Later stages of early literacy

There are several aspects of literacy that have not been discussed in this chapter and this is because they are later developments. Among these are such matters as: reading and understanding non-fiction; writing and redrafting; 'authoring' or creating stories and books; critical appreciation of literature; and handwriting. Chapter 5 is devoted to case studies of work in early years settings and will tackle some of these later stages in literacy development as they occur in the particular settings. The place of standardized spelling in the early years curriculum is, however, worth commenting on here because it is a source of much misunderstanding and confusion. A great deal of pressure can be put on early years professionals to either spell everything for beginner writers, or 'correct' their attempts at words immediately. This runs counter to the considerable knowledge about how children learn to spell that has been around for decades. A developmental pattern in children's strategies for tackling English spelling was identified by an American researcher (Gentry 1982) who re-analysed the material in a seminal case study by Glenda Bissex (1980). This analysis of developmental spelling stages still provides clues to children's growing understanding of English spelling.

Developmental spelling (Gentry 1982)

- *Desire to communicate* and share in the general writing activities of the home and community.
- *Pre-communicative* stage of spelling seen in scribbles, isolated letters and numerals and 'pretend' writing activities.
- *Semi-phonetic* stage as letter and sound relationships are explored, notably the discovery that the names of letters of the alphabet represent some sounds of spoken language, for example, 'RUDF' ('are you deaf') (Bissex 1980). These relationships are frequently exploited by children and adults in text messaging.
- *Phonetic stage* is characterized by more complete attempts to represent all the sounds of phonemes and words, for examples, 'DO NAT DSTRB GNYS AT WRK' ('do not disturb genius at work') (Bissex 1980).
- *Transition stage* to standardized spelling begins to include some conventional and historical, but *not phonetic*, features of standard English spelling, for example, 'night', 'cough', 'said'. The appearance of such patterns and letter strings is influenced by the child's wider reading and visual memory for words.
- *Standardized spelling ... the stage where we all can still make mistakes and need spell checkers – human, electronic and dictionary!*

A final thought: research suggests that the formal teaching of spelling only benefits children when they have reached the 'Transition' phase.

The role of the adult in supporting early literacy

- Adults should act as literacy informants.
- Adults should act as literacy demonstrators.
- Adults should be scribes.
- Adults should be reading partners.
- Adults should be literacy role models.
- Adults should be literacy facilitators.

The role of adults as literacy partners is crucial as young children become aware of literacy in their communities and the part it plays in the lives of their carers and families. Young children will need adults who act as *literacy informants*, telling them what print 'says', and as *literacy demonstrators* who show them how to write themselves. They also need adults as scribes who will write for them and at their dictation, adults as *reading partners* who share books with them, and adults who are *literacy role models* who value literacy and use it in their own lives. Finally, it is clear that young children need adults to be *literacy facilitators* who provide the time, opportunities and materials for literacy to happen and for children and print of all kinds to get together.

This may appear to be a fairly daunting list of roles for adults, but we do not all have to be good at all these things. We do have to be *aware* of them, and very active in cooperating to ensure that a variety of adult carers, professionals and educators together meet the children's literacy needs.

Summary

Literacy emerges from the basic human drive to represent experiences in order to 'hold' them and make some sense of them. Or, in other words, in order to think. Making marks, investigating print and beginning to write are forms of representation and they emerge early in infancy and childhood. Adults can support children's literacy development by creating the optimum conditions for learning about literacy, guiding children towards asking the right questions about print and helping children to develop their own useful strategies for tackling print. The current interest in phonics teaching must be seen in the broader context of child development, social experiences and literacy.

Provision and activities

- *Materials and tools* As indicated in the previous chapters, babies and children need books (see the starter list at the end of Chapter 3). In homes and small group settings children need easy access to collections of paper, including 'waste' paper of all kinds (computer printouts, wallpaper scraps, old diaries); card, chalkboards, offcuts of hardboard, clean paper bags, used envelopes, unused forms and applications, and so on. Larger group settings and schools will also be able to use these materials and supplement them with paper of various kinds and some blank books, although school exercise books and lined paper will impose unhelpful restrictions on young children's mark-making, experimental writing and investigations of print. Markers of many kinds should be provided, including brushes and paint, plain and coloured pencils, felt pens, biros, wax crayons, chalks and charcoal. Thick pencils and chubby crayons are not the only markers young children need – they also wish to write like grown-ups and enjoy handling fine markers and delicate colours.

- *Places* The organization of literacy materials and tools and the provision of comfortable places in which to write and read are important literacy matters. In home settings it is possible for children and carers to find their own favourite spots for reading and for small collections of books to be kept in a special corner, a box or on a shelf. Similarly, it is only necessary to keep a good collection of paper, other materials and markers in cartons, carrier bags or drawers and cupboards accessible for the children. Larger group settings must give more thought to planning literacy areas and the storage of materials for many children. Most professional carers and educators attempt to create 'literacy workshops' in their settings where the children will find plenty of books in cosy, attractive reading corners and areas; some tables and desks for writing at; perhaps a computer and software; ample collections of print from the outside world (magazines and newspapers, letters, maps, shopping lists, recipes, carrier bags, programmes, forms, cartons and labels, greetings cards, etc.); all the tools, markers and paper they need stored in carefully labelled boxes, on shelves or in baskets and other storage units. Other important materials that can support and develop early literacy are CDs and video tapes and DVDs of stories and favourite books, as well as 'story props' (discussed below).

- *Things to do* Many suggestions for early literacy work with young children have been made in the course of this chapter and it should be absolutely clear that the highest priority must be given to:
  - sharing books with children;

- telling and reading stories to them and;
- providing continual opportunities for drawing, painting, mark-making and writing.

To these basics four other early literacy activities can be added:

- making books;
- making story props;
- shared reading;
- shared writing.

Making books often happens fairly spontaneously when a child folds a sheet of paper in half and calls it 'a book'. Adults can encourage this by folding and stapling or sewing sheets of paper together. Children can draw pictures for their first books, write in them and stick in pictures, post-cards and photos. It is well worth taking photos for these books and in group settings we can make bigger books for small groups of children to record shared experiences (e.g. 'Our visit to the street market'). Families and individual carers can make books with their children that are of great personal and cultural relevance, although they may be shared with other children. Many people like to start book making with a simple zig-zag of concertina-folded strong paper or card. A few photos of relatives, holidays or previous homes can be put in a scrapbook with simple written captions, such as 'Granpa lives in Shanghai' or 'Mummy lived in this house in Delhi when she was a little girl'. Or, a book can be made about the birth of a new brother or sister or the celebration of a wedding or any other culturally significant life event. It is important that a family's own written language, apart from English, is used in these personal books. English translations can be added later if appropriate or necessary. Book making teaches chil-dren that they can be authors and raises the self-esteem of children and families (they have joined the literacy club). It also teaches the specialized language and conventions of literacy: pictures, print, pages, cover, title, author, illustrator and words.

Making story props is a way of bringing stories in books alive in a very special way for young children and also of providing them with 'props' to support their own recall and retelling of the stories. A prop can be an audio tape, or CD version of a book (particularly effective if the recording is made by a parent, carer or teacher); it can be some drawings of the characters in the book, backed with velcro or magnetic tape for moving about on a metal surface or a felt-covered board. Props can also be soft toys or puppets (a Spot, a teddy, a rag doll); and props can be objects that play a part in the book (e.g. hot water bottle, shopping basket, model dinosaurs, three spoons and three bowls).

Shared reading enables us to share a book with a group of young children so that they share their varying degrees of knowledge about narratives, books, print, words and sounds with each other. This pooling of reading knowledge is further enriched by adult readers who add their skills to the discussions and guide the children's responses by drawing their attention to details in pictures and print; for example, conventions of page layout (Where do I go next? What do I have to read?), punctuation (What is that mark for?) and recurring patterns like alliteration and rhyme. This sharing also helps children to make predictions about plot, motives and word meanings. Shared reading is now an established practice in educational settings and very large versions of many favourite children's picture books are easily available in high street bookshops. These are known as 'big books' and their size is designed to ensure that every child in a group can see the finest details of print and illustrations. Shared reading is every bit as valuable when carried out at home between children and parents or other family members.

Shared writing is more commonly practised in educational group settings and it adds to children's knowledge of the conventions of writing as they begin to move from early mark-making to experiments with signs, letters and spellings. The adult writes (acts as scribe) on a flip chart, small chalkboard or on large sheets of paper attached to a small easel and uses a bold marker pen. The group discusses what they wish to write about, and this should arise from their shared interests and experiences. The adult scribe is the children's literacy adviser and helps them to form their individual spoken contributions into linked phrases and sentences, which can be recorded in writing. This teaches the children a great deal about the differences between speech and writing. As the scribes write they share every aspect of their thinking and planning out loud with the children/authors (Where do I start? Do I use a capital letter? How do I spell that? What does it start with? Do I put a full stop now?). The children can see how a text grows, what decisions writers have to make, why conventions of punctuation and spelling are so important and why it is essential to rewrite things to make our meanings absolutely clear.

Further reading

Browne, A. (2007) *Teaching and Learning Communication, Language and Literacy*. London: Paul Chapman.

Campbell, R. (1999) *Literacy from Home to School: Reading with Alice*. Stoke-on-Trent: Trentham Books.

Featherstone, S. (ed.) (2006) *L is for Sheep – Getting Ready for Phonics*. Lutterworth: Featherstone Education.

Hall, N. and Robinson, A. (2003) *Exploring Writing and Play in the Early Years*, 2nd edn. London: David Fulton.

Kress, G. (1996) *Before Writing: Rethinking the Paths to Literacy*. London: Routledge.

Kress, G. (2000) *Early Spelling: Between Convention and Creativity*. London: Routledge.

Miller, L. (1996) *Towards Reading*. Buckingham: Open University Press.

Language, literature and literacy in early years settings: case studies

> These schools are communities, mutual communities of learners/
> doers/imaginers, all engaged in exploring the world of the possible,
> constructing new experiences. Not only children and teachers, but also
> families, and even interested visitors like me . . . Everybody is lending a
> hand, doing a job, trying to make sense. It is a community of mutual
> interest – a model of what a community based on respect should be,
> where everything develops through interactive processes of
> continuous negotiation between different perspectives and points of
> view . . . This is what I found in the infant-toddler centers and
> preschools of Reggio Emilia.
>
> (Bruner 1996: 117)

This chapter focuses on:

• case studies of the communication, language and literacy curriculum in
  three early years settings in the maintained and private sectors.

The achievements and commitment of the children and the communities
that support the Reggio Emilia early years schools in Italy cannot be too
highly praised and they are a source of inspiration to practitioners and
families around the world. The case studies which make up this chapter
are a reminder that we do not necessarily have to travel to Italy in order to
find early years settings that are communities of respect where children,
teachers, families, helpers and visitors are learners, doers and imaginers.

The settings chosen are a state-maintained nursery school and Children's Centre in north London, some private sector schools that are part of an international philosophical and educational movement, the Rudolf Steiner Waldorf Schools (usually referred to as Steiner Waldorf Education), and a maintained integrated Early Years Centre in East Anglia. These case studies of early years education 'in action' are examples of actual practice and attempt to capture the essence of what goes on, 'catching the moments' as it were, somewhat like the child observations scattered through the previous chapters. Of course it is not simply a matter of describing the 'happenings'; it is equally important to try and gain some insights into what the 'doers' themselves – children and adults – think about what they are doing, feeling, making and experiencing.

Hampden Way Nursery School

Some background information

Hampden Way Nursery School is situated in a residential area of north London where the residents are mostly home owners, although a small percentage of the children attending the school live in local authority rented accommodation. The building was put up during the Second World War as a temporary day nursery for the young children of munitions workers.

There are two classrooms of similar size connected by a bathroom area; a front entrance conservatory with a book area for both adults and children; a staffroom; a small kitchen; three offices; an extended day area with its own outdoor provision; and a Children's Centre, also with its own outdoor provision. The main school outdoor area has a sloping garden with grassed and tarmac areas, reached from the rear of the building by stone steps and a slope. The two areas immediately outside each classroom are roofed over to provide a sheltered play space in wet weather. During hot weather the children are protected by two enormous sunshades that are static.

Hampden Way is an extended school so we also offer full day care from 8 a.m. to 6 p.m., toddler groups, toy library, postnatal groups, dental health sessions and motor skills programmes. Our services are extending rapidly as we develop the Children's Centre programme.

The outside garden area is viewed as an integral and complementary part of the learning environment and is always developing and extending. The permanent facilities include a large sandpit, two dig pits for children – one with bark chippings and one with mud – so they can experience different media, a small pond, a swing frame with tyres and wooden boards, a pergola, a large wooden train, a raised stage area and a large house-like structure incorporating a slide.

There are 100 children on role, 50 attending the morning sessions and 50 attending the afternoon sessions, including 24 children who attend full time. The children and their families encompass the rich social and cultural diversity found in all large cities, but the largest ethnic minority group is Asian (17.46 per cent) and 36 per cent of these children enter the school with little or no English but on leaving are usually competent in understanding and speaking English. Children are admitted twice yearly and their ages on entry range from 3 years and 1 month to 3 years and 8 months, and many leave well before their fifth birthday to enter local primary schools.

The school staff consists of three teachers (including the head and her class-based deputy), four nursery nurses (two nursery nurses are a job share post), two full-time welfare assistants working with children who have been identified as having a need or a designated special educational need, one Ethnic Minority Grant (EMA) assistant, two part-time school secretaries, three mealtime supervisors, three extended day workers and a site supervisor.

The practitioners in this school would probably describe themselves as working in the well-established traditions of British nursery education, with its strong emphasis on knowledge of child development and the provision of a developmentally appropriate curriculum in the early years. This includes viewing the *processes* of learning as of great significance, rather than focusing exclusively on narrow outcomes or results. It is an approach often described as 'child-centred', although many practitioners prefer to call it learner-centred or even 'child-sensitive' (Bredekamp and Rosegrant 1992).

This commitment to developmentally appropriate practice (Bredekamp 1987) at Hampden Way is reflected in the organization of teaching, material resources and the school environment. The latter is organized around curriculum resource areas spanning both classrooms, although a book area is included in both rooms. The children have access to a language and literacy area, a listening area, an arts workshop (incorporating woodwork), science and mathematics areas, sand and water provision, large block play and small construction areas, a music area, a home corner, small-world play, malleable materials, computers, ICT resources and an interactive whiteboard, plus all the resources of the garden. Children are encouraged to use the resources throughout the school, take care of them and use them appropriately. The staff aim to foster the children's independence and encourage them to make connections in their learning, recognizing that 'learning is not compartmentalized' in the early years.

The whole staff team works on a rota basis covering both rooms and the garden, and while the teachers lead the teams the nursery nurses participate fully in all aspects of the school's organization and practice.

The broad approach to language and literacy

Staff are constantly developing their own knowledge and skills in supporting children's language and literacy development, analysing their current practices and drawing up plans to ensure that this fundamental area is fostered most effectively. The following written comments by the previous and the current headteacher set out the school's broad approach to language and literacy:

A wealth of observations of children talking, representing and playing have informed our practice, together with research evidence and case studies of young children that draw on evidence from a wide variety of cultural and social backgrounds (Torrey 1973; Heath 1983; Bissex 1984; Payton 1984). All this research and knowledge convinced us that children are active in constructing their own theories about language. They ask questions of themselves, as well as of adults, using situational [everyday] print as a resource. Although not directly instructed, children are supported by adults who talk with them, responding to their questions and offering further information.

Vygotsky (1978) refers to the 'zone of proximal development' that looks at a child's current stage of development and at the level of her [sic] potential development that can be achieved with appropriate guidance and support from adults. We believe that it is a question of 'tuning in' to children and enabling them to take the next step forward in their learning. Bruner (1983) called this 'scaffolding' children's learning.

The guiding principles for the school's practice that emerged from our discussions of research and practice were that children should:

- be active participants in their own learning;
- have their own learning strategies and experience valued, supported and extended;
- have many opportunities to interact with sensitive and supportive adults;
- have many opportunities for play and talk;
- be in an environment that reflects their social and cultural identities;
- be in an environment that is rich in a wide variety of print;
- have access to ICT as a means of communication;
- be in an environment that values their comments;
- see their ideas and thoughts reflected in their learning environment;

- be encouraged to use non-verbal gestures;
- develop their language and literacy in a meaningful and integrated way.

Many conflicting theories about the ways in which children learn are now current. For example, too early an emphasis is often being placed on the formation of neat regularly formed letters. Yet it is the process of learning that is of fundamental importance. Bissex refers to the 'child's inner teacher' (1984). Children's learning needs to be skilfully supported and extended, or 'scaffolded', so that their own very effective structures that enable them to experiment, predict, test, amend and construct rules can flourish. In other words, we must have faith in the child.

Speaking and listening

The school strives to create a setting in which children can talk freely with each other and with adults in spontaneous conversations and through role play. The provision of such things as play telephones, walkie talkies and an outdoor telephone kiosk provide opportunities for talking and listening in a variety of real-life situations. This little girl shown in Figure 5.1 is making a telephone call to her nan. She has looked up her phone number in the telephone directory and then has called her to ask the number of her house. In this nursery setting opportunities for private one-to-one conversations between adult and child are seen as vitally important and professional educators, students, visitors and parents can be found talking to children. The children are given time to talk, to think aloud and find and experiment with words.

This careful planning for collaborative talk and listening between children and between adults and children reflects the professional staff's understanding that talk is of fundamental importance in all areas of children's learning as well as being the foundation of literacy. Guidance on a wide range of provision and activities for talking and listening and on what adults can do to support it is displayed in a portfolio of examples for communication, language and literacy created especially for parents and other professionals by the staff.

Stories, storytelling and books

The children are given many opportunities to experience the joy of stories. Stories are read and told at group story times at the end of sessions and are also told and read on request to individuals or small groups during the course of the day. Story sessions include poetry, rhyme and songs as the children love to play with words, hear them rhyming in poems and nonsense rhymes and create their own verses, jingles and tongue-twisters.

Figure 5.1 A phone call to nan.

The children are given many opportunities to look at books independently so that they can view themselves as readers, or take on the role of story-tellers with their friends, or just retreat from the demands of group life. In Figure 5.2 we see two girls sharing a story together. They already have a love of books and the link to the story book table enables them to retell the story and act it out using props.

Books are everywhere in the school and children can be found reading to each other round every corner, often interrupting their play to browse through a favourite book or create a fantastic tale from the pictures. In this literary early years setting it is not unusual to see a child, dressed in all the glory of an old bridesmaid's dress, put down her doll baby and big handbag, put her feet up on a stool and have a quiet 'read'. Similarly, two 4-year-old 'space travellers' paused in their explorations of the universe to read books to each other, while still keeping their helmets on – ready for the next 'lift off'.

Figure 5.2 Sharing a story and using story props.

In a setting so permeated by stories, role play, books and the love of literature it is not surprising to find the stories the children know constantly recreated by them, with the aid of story props, which enable them to understand, recall and re-enact texts. Most props are made by the staff, but a few are purchased and some are improvised by the children. The story props for *Whatever Next* (see Figure 5.3) were set up in the cottage. The cottage had been converted into a rocket ship by the staff because the story was such a favourite with the children and they were very interested in space and the universe. The children enacted the story using the same props as the bear in the story and varying the pitch of their own voices to indicate different characters.

The children regularly hear stories and rhymes in languages other than English. This is because parents are asked to come in and share their languages and literary culture with the children. Families are also given a CD or audio tape to add the children's favourite music from their own cultures. Clearly this is an aspect of working in partnership with families and the community (see Chapter 7), but it also indicates that the school values ethnic, cultural and linguistic diversity. These kinds of experience

Figure 5.3 Playing with the story props for *Whatever Next*.

enrich the language curriculum and demonstrate the school's respect for what families and children bring to the educational process.

Books are available throughout the school, including the entrance, the hallway and imaginative play areas like the 'home corner'. Here there are books, magazines, comics and written materials that the children might find in their own homes. The staff choose books that will reflect aspects of the children's own backgrounds and experiences, as well as the traditional tales of many cultures and the wilder fantasies of many modern picture books. They also look for repetitive texts and pop-up devices that encourage attention, prediction, memorization and an awareness of the permanent features of written texts. Before reading a book the staff make a point of referring to the book's author and illustrator so that the children can appreciate that real people write and illustrate books. There is also a dedicated area in one of the classrooms where books by favourite authors and illustrators are displayed. The children are encouraged to make their own books – either individually or in groups – and the themes often arise from a favourite story book or a special experience. Some children dictate their own story to a member of staff who writes it down, some make marks or draw pictures for their books, and some use their own developmental writing strategies to create text. It is not surprising that at Hampden Way stories spill over into all aspects of the curriculum, as when a group of children exploring the local park set off through the 'swishy swashy' long grass announcing that they were 'going on a bear hunt'. Or when three children playing on the horizontal ladder of the climbing frame became the Three Billy Goats Gruff 'trip trapping' over the bridge.

Play

The fact that stories and books become fully integrated into the children's imaginative play has already been indicated, and the school's provision of everyday written materials in the home corner, as well as play 'office' areas with telephones, notepads, stationery and directories confirms an approach to literacy, which is thoughtful and play-based. The power and fascination of literacy is demonstrated in many examples of the children's play:

- clip boards in various areas to encourage children to use their emergent writing strategies;
- plastic magnetic letters, wooden letters, stamps, painting and drawing materials – often used to incorporate letters and numerals in patterns, scribbles and representational pictures;
- spontaneous use of a sharp tool to make letter-like marks on flattened clay, as well as the formation of the letters of a child's name from rolled 'worms' of clay;
- buckets of water and decorating brushes put in the garden for children who 'painted' the outside apparatus 'in role' as decorators. Children wrote their names and also did representational drawings of themselves and their families;
- all the malleable materials are used to practise emergent writing.

The use of large blocks and bricks also has its literacy dimension as writing materials are always available nearby and the children often draw and write about their constructions. Interpreting and using symbols of many kinds is a fundamental aspect of literacy development.

Emergent writing and reading

The gradual emergence of young children's literacy understandings and skills out of real needs to read and write and meaningful experiences of literacy in action are amply demonstrated by all these examples. The staff of this nursery school do not leave the emergence of literacy to chance but plan for it and nurture it. The children are given the tools that adults use and the staff themselves are 'models' of literate people because they take care to read and write in front of the children (doing office work with the door open; looking at a book while the children settle down for a story session). The nursery environment is rich in print: there are calendars, food boxes and newspapers in the home corner; school signs and information are written in the several home languages of the children; labels on the equipment are made by the children as well as the staff; and the children have their own name labels to use purposefully. For example, they 'register' for each session by placing their names on a table as they arrive and place their milk carton next to their name. The children have name tags in the communication, language and literacy and creative areas so they can use them as useful and significant resources and references all through the session. There is also a dedicated Makaton area and the children are taught a new Makaton sign each week and the parents have a Makaton sign board so they too know the sign of the week.

Just as literacy serves real purposes for the adults and children in this nursery, so the children themselves are treated as readers and writers from the beginning. They are not in any 'pre-' stage and their initial mark-making is treated as part of a learning continuum that, if 'scaffolded' appropriately, will lead to conventional writing and reading with understanding. All the stages of the children's mark-making and writing are displayed in the school to show the children that their work is valued and to help their parents understand the developmental processes of literacy. Even the displayed alphabet frieze, which can be a helpful reference point for young readers and writers, is particularly meaningful because it has been made up from the children's photos and first names:

Dd   Dimitri   Damon   Daniel   Dario   Diane

Reading and writing for real purposes – some snapshots

Michael is a piano player and he was well aware that music has a written language of its own. He requested some notation paper so that he could produce his own music. He went and found a music book that he could use as a reference when drawing his quavers and crochets (see Figure 5.4).

Mawluda (4 years 1 month) drew some interesting 'boxes' after watching the teacher mark the register (see Figure 5.5). Mawluda is from Afghanistan, her first language is Farsi and, as yet, she speaks very little English. On the day that she apparently represented the distinctive format of the school register, she also created the written communication

Figure 5.4 Michael writes music.

Figure 5.5 Mawluda's 'register'.

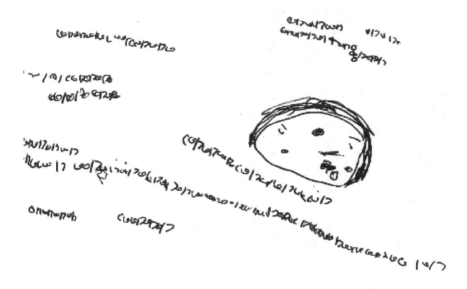

Figure 5.6 Mawluda's writing.

shown in Figure 5.6. The written forms of Farsi may well be influencing her early writing as other examples of her daily spontaneous writing, including tiny drawings, indicated. It is clear that Mawluda uses written forms to make sense of the puzzling new world of school, to explore the potential of written communications and to engage in an important high-status activity.

Maximillian had been digging for worms in the garden. He then decided he wanted to make a poster and record how many worms he had found. Maximillian is a reader and can break down words phonetically so he was able to listen to the sounds in the word and write it down, adding a number '3' for the amount of worms he had collected (Figure 5.7).

ICT and literacy

ICT is an integral part of the nursery school and is used for many purposes. Children have the opportunity to use ICT as a means of communication. In this example, Sophie had had enough of the poor weather and decided to send an email to the weather lady. Sophie used her knowledge of sounds to write her message phonetically. It reads, 'Dear Weather Lady, Can you make the rain go away, just a few showers, Love, Sophie'.

Dr wr lad
Can u mac f ran go aw jast a fw sws
Lav Sophie
Xxxx

Figure 5.7 Max's 3 worms poster.

Michael had sent the following email to the headteacher from his home. He had attached two photos of himself; one dressed up as a doctor and the other one was of him singing a song in French. He had sent this email independently and had written the message by himself using his knowledge of phonics. Michael became a proficient user of email and sent messages and pictures home to his family, as well as to the headteacher at school.

Mee being u doctdu and sing ing u frech song
From Michael

Children have access to talking photo albums and postcards and use these with staff to record events at home and at the nursery. These are very effective in terms of speaking and listening and allow the children to use their own experiences and make them come to life through their personal photos and dialogue.

The children also have access to microphones, digital cameras, video cameras, karaoke machines, CD players, metal detectors and notebooks. The children use the interactive whiteboard where their pictures are shown on a rolling slide show so that they can talk about their photos. The adults are also able to make talking picture books with the children, using their work and their photos.

The use of ICT has enabled the school to involve the parents more in their children's learning.

Records and assessment

The staff plan carefully for the development of the children's language and literacy, in the classrooms and in the garden (Appendix II), and this planning is shaped by detailed records of the children's progress and interests. Profiles of individual children are built up using information gained through:

- ongoing discussions with parents (initiated on a home visit);
- child observations (both planned and targeted at individuals, and spontaneous);
- collected samples of children's work (drawings, paintings, writing, photos);
- Blue profile books. These are the children's books and they are used as a self-assessment tool. The children make the decisions about what goes into the books and there is lots of discussion on a one-to-one basis with an adult about their work and photos;
- observations by parents.

Individual reviews of progress take place termly and are shared with parents. Final profiles, written in the child's last term, are also created in partnership with parents and forwarded to the appropriate primary school.

Children are observed regularly throughout their period in the school. Staff meet together weekly to discuss 'targeted' children and to share the parents' observations as a whole staff team and plan for the next steps for each individual child.

After approximately six weeks newly admitted children's records will be analysed to provide an early assessment of their present stage of learning, ongoing development and attainment on entry. Areas of concern can be identified and development more closely monitored. Caution is adopted in all these early assessment procedures in order to minimize hasty and inappropriate judgements.

Steiner Waldorf Education

Some background notes[1]

Steiner Waldorf is an international educational movement with some schools, kindergartens and teacher training institutes in most countries. The general philosophy reflects a central European tradition of valuing childhood for its own sake, but the movement's direct inspiration is found in the writings of the Austrian philosopher Rudolf Steiner (1861–1925). The emphasis of the approach is developmental with three distinctive stages of childhood recognized and supported by an appropriate curriculum: early years (0–7), childhood (7–14) and adolescence and early adulthood (14–21). These stages connect with a threefold 'hand, heart and head' concept of education that relates to the development of the corresponding faculties of willing, feeling and thinking in the individual. In the first phase the emphasis is on the *will*. The children first encounter the world through their own willed bodily activity and gradually acquire a repertoire of increasingly refined skills as movement and coordination are brought under control. In the second phase the affective or *feeling* realm predominates and the third phase culminates in the development of mature adult *thinking*.

The early years phase is seen as a period of active learning in which children play and imitate, absorb and reflect on their experiences in a secure, caring and structured environment. Teaching is always by example rather than instruction at this stage. There is a clear moral and spiritual – although undenominational – emphasis and a strong belief in social responsibility, routine and community. The curriculum is planned so as to be sensitive to the developmental needs of the individual child and play is valued as a significant mode of learning during this period when children 'think' with their entire being. The need to grasp things physically (with the will) is a precursor to the later grasping of concepts (with the thinking). Only when new capabilities for abstract thinking appear at around the seventh year are children considered to be physically, emotionally and intellectually ready for formal instruction.

The aims and objectives outlined in the Steiner Waldorf early years curriculum statement are:

- to recognize and support each stage of child development;
- to provide opportunities for children to be active in meaningful imitation;
- to work with rhythm and repetition;
- to encourage personal, social and moral development;
- to provide an integral learning experience;

- to encourage creative play and to support physical development;
- to encourage children to know and love the natural and human world;
- to provide a safe, child-friendly environment;
- to work with parents as the child's main educators.

Most of these aims are familiar enough to parents and early years workers but two are less so and need expanding. The notion of 'meaningful imitation' relates to the Steiner view that young children learn by example, by imitating and modelling their behaviour on what goes on around them. Thus a Steiner kindergarten is a community of 'doers', whether it be baking their own bread or cleaning a room, and it follows that adult carers and workers must always strive to be worthy of imitation (both morally and practically). This is not a naive theory of mindless copying but an awareness of the complex ways in which the young need to be involved and initiated into the ways of their communities.

Working with 'rhythm and repetition' indicates the central role played by rhythm in Steiner Waldorf educational principles. At one level this is reflected in the high priority given to music and poetic language in Steiner schools, but it goes deeper. Children are seen to need the reassurance of continuity and regularity, so great stress is put on such orderly rituals as activity and rest times, tidying up and 'ring times' (for songs, poetry, movement and circle games), stories, seasonal celebrations and birthdays. These rhythmic patterns help children to live with change, find their place in the world and begin to understand the past, present and future. Repetition is seen to strengthen memory and establish continuity and, in the case of stories and rhymes, gives the children many opportunities to become familiar with new material and reflect on its meanings.

In the UK there are many Steiner Waldorf kindergartens, schools and teacher training organizations (www.steinerwaldorf.org.uk). Most of the material in the following case study came from the Rosebridge Steiner Kindergarten in Cambridge (which has now moved onto the same premises as the all-through Steiner school). The kindergarten occupied the ground floor of a converted house and had a garden with a paved area, a sandpit, a gardening area and space for play and large constructions. This area was equipped with planks, steps, branches and logs that the children used to build see-saws, slides, ever-changing obstacle courses and even a merry-go-round. Figure 5.8 shows children building and improvising with similar materials in the Christchurch Gardens Kindergarten in Reading.

At Rosebridge there was an organic vegetable garden created and worked with the parents. This produced vegetables and fruit, not only to eat but to sell for kindergarten funds. There is evidence of lots of

Figure 5.8 Building in the garden.

domestic and imaginative play, cooking and baking, provision for music, drawing and painting, wax and clay modelling and 'endless construction' (a teacher's words) using large blocks, wooden screens for house building, as well as small dolls and unformed wooden toys (toys that are multi-use, requiring imagination) used to create miniature worlds. There were also tables, chairs and garden equipment. Rhythm and ritual are established by having a weekly pattern of activities: Monday is baking day, Tuesday is painting, Wednesday is crafts, Thursday is cooking and Friday is cleaning and polishing. The seasons of the year are celebrated and this includes the great festivals of Easter, May Day, Harvest, Michaelmas, Diwali and Christmas. A very great occasion is made of every child's birthday, with a crown to wear and candles, flowers, cake, birthday verses and the participation of the parents.

The broad approach to language and literacy

The Steiner Waldorf early years curriculum is a totally integrated one and any attempt to separate out the elements of language and literacy distorts the full picture. Therefore the following comments from an experienced practitioner and adviser (Jenkinson 1997a) focus on the philosophy and principles that shape developmentally appropriate education in Steiner Waldorf kindergartens.

Contemporary life puts children under increasing pressure to grow up as quickly as possible and current research shows that children in coercive early learning programmes suffer from high levels of anxiety, stress, sleep problems and low self-esteem. Forcing children to learn skills before they are maturationally ready is both ineffective and counterproductive. Full perceptual processing ability is not complete in a child of four years old and we respect the process of gradual development which allows the aural and visual senses to mature slowly over time ... We feel that accelerated formal learning is achieved at a cost – and our concern is that 'hot house' children may prove to be less robust in the long term. We believe that each stage of child development has unique qualities to impart to the child and should be experienced fully before the next stage is embarked upon.

We concentrate on pre-literacy and pre-numeracy skills, skills which are 'caught rather than taught', our children have good phonological awareness, their oral skills are strong, their vocabulary is extensive and by their seventh year they are ready and physiologically *able* to learn. By creating a friendly environment, where each child feels safe and not under pressure to perform, the kindergarten teacher weaves a tapestry of learning experiences for the child – all the elements of which have context and meaning and arise from the life of the kindergarten itself. Through familiar events, which make sense to the children, at *their* level – and which relate to the well-ordered kindergarten daily, weekly and yearly rhythms – children cook, bake, garden, paint, draw; they listen quietly – out of interest rather than compulsion – to stories told to them by their teachers, they celebrate festivals together and they learn to consider the needs of others. They learn for life from life. All learning is practical and substantive. Our children do involve themselves in activities such as making their own books; many write their names and a few discover reading, but most are busy with their own 'serious work' and we support their self-initiated activity. To quote Rousseau, 'What is the use of inscribing on their brains a list of symbols which mean nothing to them? They will learn the symbols when they learn the things signified'.

(Rousseau [1762] 1991: 76)

Talking and listening

Steiner kindergartens take a particular approach to talking and listening in the early years curriculum. The emphasis is on listening to and developing an appreciation for live music (lyre, flute, human voice); listening to traditional stories and stories created from daily experiences; learning songs and singing games with mimed and verbal responses; creating role-play scenarios and drama; recalling experiences and developing narrative and conversational skills; performing puppet shows; and reciting nursery rhymes to develop the rhythms of language and a feeling for sound and melody.

The musical and poetic qualities of language are emphasized by the use of verses and rhymes to mark the daily, seasonal and celebratory routines of kindergarten life. Thus a retelling of a traditional fairy tale may be preceded by a familiar song that sets the mood and encourages listening:

Mother of the fairy tale take me by your silver hand,
Sail me in your silver boat, sail me silently afloat.
Mother of the fairy tale take me to your shining land.

And a very popular blessing is usually sung before meals:

Blessings on the blossom, blessings on the fruit,
Blessings on the leaf and stem, blessings on the root.

After this blessing adults and children all join hands around the table and say together 'Blessings on the meal'.

Undoubtedly the use of language in Steiner schools is marked by attention to gesture, well-formulated speech and musicality, but there is also a remarkable liveliness and playfulness in the spontaneous conversations of children with each other and with adults. Some examples of play with language will be returned to in the comments on 'Play', but a few snippets of conversations will demonstrate the intellectual and social power of the oral curriculum in these kindergartens. Like young children everywhere they talk during meals, while they play, while they tidy up and while they cook. In this first example a group of children are baking Christmas biscuits at Wynstones Kindergarten in Gloucester.

Child 1:	We're making patterns on these biscuits.
Child 2:	We're having licks afterwards.
Joshua (5):	We're not allowed to lick until we've done every single one.

A later conversation in the same school between Joshua (5) and a little girl (4) reveals both true logic (using if/then clauses) and a Hamlet-like awareness of folk myths and family loyalty:

Joshua: Ghosts are people who have just died.
Girl: My grandfather's just died.
Joshua: Then he must be a ghost.
        Pause
Joshua: Ghosts are bad.
Girl: My grandfather wasn't bad.
Joshua: Then he won't be a ghost then, if you're bad you're a ghost.

As in all early years settings, the children frequently engage the adults in conversations that are creative and thought-provoking. The following exchange was recorded by Sally Jenkinson, Early Years Adviser, Steiner Education UK, in a personal communication:

A 4-year-old boy, Charles, asked me to come outside to see his 'bout'.

Sally: What do you mean Charles, what is a 'bout'?
Charles: It's a'bout'.
Sally: Do you mean a belt to put round your waist?
Charles: No, I mean a 'bout'.

At this point Charles decided I just wasn't getting it, so he took me to the sandpit where a straight line and a circle had been carefully shaped out of the sand.

Charles: Look Sally [said with polite exasperation] it's a *round*-a bout.

Once I saw it, it all made sense. Relief and triumph were written all over Charles' face: I have made her understand – at last! It was as if a 'bout' were a place where things met and changed, a place where there might indeed be other kinds of bout: square bouts, or oblong bouts, for example. (We do have the expressions 'about turn' and 'thereabouts', so perhaps Charles was on to something.) He had a basic concept that a 'bout', as a noun, somehow stayed still whilst things happened in different ways around it, and he was intuitively following the rules of grammar which apply when adjectives describe nouns. Charles was searching for a way to name the (empty) space. This deeply thoughtful boy's father was an architect.

Stories, storytelling and books

The oral telling of stories and the development of children's narrative skills are major features of Steiner Waldorf education and although the formal teaching of reading is not begun until children are 6-plus, picture books with little or no text are used in some kindergartens. Sometimes a teacher will share a special book with a group of children and it is not unusual to find children looking at picture books and telling their own stories. Morning stories, however, are always 'told' rather than read to the children.

In another personal communication Sally Jenkinson writes:

> An important feature of the kindergarten day is the story. The stories are drawn from a wide range of folk and fairy tales, as well as nature and seasonal stories (which follow the cycle of the year), stories about plants and animals, and stories of families and domestic life.
>
> The telling of a story is always a special event in the kindergarten day. Traditionally the telling of folk tales marked the coming of night and created in the mind a different rhythm. Our stories are told to the whole kindergarten group and are sometimes acted out with gesture, song and movement in circle time. The beautifully chosen words, well-constructed narratives and deep underlying structures and patterns in the traditional tales are the child's first introduction to literature. We observe little customs such as lighting a candle, singing a special song or playing some lyre music, as a prelude to the story and to help the children leave the work of the day and enter the realm of the imagination.
>
> The fairy stories are told because they paint beautiful pictures of our human feelings, as personified by the greedy wolf, the honest miller's son, the courageous youngest prince; they tell of trickery, treachery, cruelty and folly and give an overview of life. All the characters in one story make up a whole because all qualities, good and bad and everything in between, are an essential part of human nature . . . potential aspects of our own being.
>
> Fairy tales also give the child access to a rich vocabulary of words and concepts. A 3-year-old child in the Wynstones Kindergarten, Gloucester, demonstrated her ability to make meaning out of her morning story by creating a new context to try out the words and phrases she had heard earlier. She took a little stand-up puppet doll and began to retell the story. As she carefully moved her puppet, who represented the good girl in the story, she was heard to say in a voice of great precision and emphasis and not without a dramatic flourish, 'She

was a *paragon* of virtue . . .'. This small storyteller may not know the meanings of the individual words, but her understanding comes from the context in which she first heard the adult using them and now she uses them herself in her own speech, effortlessly demonstrating Bruner's 'scaffolding' and Vygotsky's 'zone of proximal development'.

It is not surprising to find the kind of fairy tale inspiration described above spilling over into all aspects of play in Steiner kindergartens and creating a complex web of the fantastic, the symbolic and the practical. In Figure 5.9 the two 4-year-old girls are princes dressed in capes and crowns, and they are feeding their horses. They had made their horses a sleeping corner with muslin representing hay and a large part of the game was taken up with discussions about what horses eat, how they sleep, how they should be cared for, and so on. The princes, Hester and Anna,

Figure 5.9 Princes feeding their horses.

wondered whether horses liked oats, hay or chestnuts. Having decided upon chestnuts they let the conkers in the basket remain as conkers (*horse-chestnuts*) and gave them to the horses as food.

Children in Steiner kindergartens are also very experienced in the crucial early literacy skill of creating a narrative, or story, about their own lives and families. This is supported by the practice of telling birthday stories. These are told on a child's birthday in the kindergarten (parents are invited and asked to supply all the crucial pre-kindergarten data), and incorporate personal biographical details into an ongoing story of the child's life. Sometimes an item from babyhood is brought in to illustrate the story and demonstrate how much the child has grown and developed in a few years. The story is brought up to date with the child's recent achievements in the kindergarten. The story is a warm celebration of the life of a child that can contribute to a sense of self-worth which lasts for years.

Steiner Waldorf early years educators would argue that care and respect for books in their kindergartens are promoted by having only a few at a time in a special area of the room. Respect is encouraged by the adults' care of books and by such practices as wrapping a treasured book in its own special cloth to keep it safe. There is usually a parents' library in which books are available for loan and the children are familiar with this. Books are used extensively in the later stages of Steiner education.

Play

'In our Steiner Waldorf Kindergartens, we are conscious of the very real threat to the world of the child and our concern is always to do the right thing at the right time – we recognise that children need time to play during their formative years' (Jenkinson 1997b: 48). This recognition is based on the widely accepted psychological theory that in play young children actually think by internalizing the processes of physical activities. Children's characteristic doing and thinking transform the most ordinary objects that come to hand into symbols, which are rich in meanings: 'The ability to endow an object with a different order of existence is a genuine childhood talent' (Jenkinson 1997c: 105). A Steiner kindergarten will be full of playing children who improvise and talk about a range of narrative possibilities. For example:

- playing cafés and 'writing' menus;
- drawing maps and signposts for various games;
- writing 'letters' to each other on leaves in the garden;
- playing offices, with kindergarten chairs and tables positioned at different angles to create 'computers', 'cash registers', 'desks', and so on;

- using pine cones as 'telephones' and nuts, seeds and shells as 'money', and even making and signing paper credit cards.

Sometimes a play sequence develops into a large-scale event that gradually involves all the children in a cooperative fantasy. An example is shown in Figure 5.10. Caitlin (4 years 5 months), in the foreground, is making 'smoke' by carding wool and George (3 years 4 months) is steering the train by rotating a circular piece of wood. Other children had cut tickets from card and sold them in exchange for conker 'money'. There was a signalman with a stop–go board of correctly coloured circles (green and red) made by the children, and a guard's flag, also child-made. The children had gone on to make special tickets for going to Africa – yellow 'because it's hot', and to London – blue 'because it's cold'. This interesting sensitivity to appropriate colour symbolism in their representations went side-by-side with a very practical approach to planning journeys: a café was opened to serve drinks and fish and chips to passengers. Once the train was under

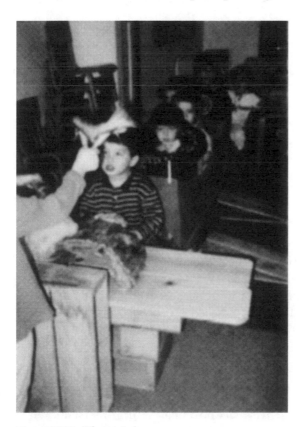

Figure 5.10 'The train'.

way all the children made the loud and necessary 'choo-choo' noises and a real bell was rung as the train approached the station and when it was about to leave.

Play can also be very quiet and intense and only involve one or two players. Adam (4 years 6 months) and Katie (3 years 4 months) were witnessed preparing dinner in their pretend house, but this was part of an extended game that had begun with shops. Katie had been shopping and bought the fish and some chips (clothes pegs) and the two children made their own house and began preparing food. They talked about cooking methods: should the fish be fried, baked, roasted or barbecued? Barbecuing won and they made an elaborate cooking rack from a wooden circle across which they wound wool. The rack was placed over a 'fire' of red sheep's wool and conkers.

Play with language and a well-developed oral and phonological sensitivity can be found in many young children who attend Steiner Waldorf schools. Sally Jenkinson again:

> ... 'the word' is created anew by every child. In the child's world, trees come 'timbering' down, caravans are 'car-wheel-housies', 'sheeps' live in fields and 'biscetti' is delicious with tomato sauce. (The same group called my assistant, who was tall, lanky but stately, 'Jean bean Elizabeth the Queen'!) In our kindergartens we hear children playing with language. They reverse words, they rhyme, they play with alliterative and onomatopoeic sounds and they create the most wonderful nonsense verse; they do this as naturally as they play with the shells and conkers around them.

Playfulness with language, and with people, comes through in the following observation:

> I sat next to a friendly boy who introduced himself to me by telling me that his name was 'M.O.T.' and that he was a car. I said that I thought he must be a very safe car. His friend, sitting nearby, turned to me with a withering look and said 'His name's Tom really ... that's M.O.T. backwards.' The two boys took great pleasure in their good-natured jest, especially as I had been so effectively caught out.
>
> (Jenkinson 1997a)

Emergent writing and reading

Although kindergarten teachers place no demands upon their children to produce letters or numbers, these often emerge spontaneously. The morning I visited the kindergarten was full of letter writing which the children were keen to show me, particularly when the window misted over, making an irresistible writing surface: 'This is my name, and this is mummy's name.' 'That's an A.' 'Those are my letters.' Numbers also scored well; fingers were spontaneously used to denote their owners' ages and children sang along with the teacher's counting rhymes. They took *great* pleasure in the alliteration and onomatopoeia of that morning's 'slithery slippery snake' rhyme.

(Jenkinson 1997a)

The above incidents in a Steiner Waldorf kindergarten could be repeated daily in any number of early years settings and private homes, but Steiner educators choose not to teach young children to 'link sounds to letters, naming and sounding the letters of the alphabet', or 'write their own names ... and begin to form simple sentences, sometimes using punctuation' (DfES 2007a). However, the children are familiar with the uses of writing in meaningful and important contexts such as their names on paintings, drawings, coat pegs and containers; the words of songs, verses and special books, or the many letters and notices for parents and teachers as well as other environmental print. On one occasion in the Sunlands Kindergarten, Stroud, two 4-year-olds had played together all morning and cooperated on a drawing of themselves. Esther (4 years 5 months) did most of it but Zoe (4 years 8 months) added her black hair, although she is a redhead, and black rain. Zoe then wrote the story on the back of the drawing: 'We went for a walk and it's raining and Tag [her dog] went in the pond'.

At this point in a child's literacy development the Steiner approach is distinctive.

It is at this stage that many educators begin to work directly with the child's emergent thinking and begin to teach literacy skills. The Steiner pre-school teacher, however, presses on with spoken language for longer, strengthening and enriching the foundations of the child's 'inner speech' (thought) so that the shift in the child's thinking which is necessary for the achievement of literacy (what psycholinguists call the shift to a 'metalinguistic consciousness') occurs from an enriched and strengthened position after approximately 7 years of age.

(Alwyn 1997: 23)

Emergent writing is supported in the Rosebridge Kindergarten in that if children ask for words the teachers will write them, but the greater emphasis is placed on lots of drawing and painting activities. They also do sewing, weaving, finger knitting, plaiting, modelling, candle-making, gardening and woodwork. All these activities are considered good for developing eye–hand coordination, fine motor skills and later reading. The kindergarten, in common with all Steiner Waldorf schools, uses traditional German block wax crayons that give strong clear colours, can be easily grasped by small hands and can be used to create broad bands of colour or angled to produce curves and fine lines. After kindergarten, children in Class 1 of Steiner schools are taught literacy in a structured progression, beginning writing with the drawing of curves and straight lines and moving on to capital letters. Alphabetic letter forms are introduced by combining the shapes of consonants into representational drawings that provide phonological and visual clues, but also involve a story about each letter. For example, 'C' may be drawn as a cave and a narrative, perhaps about who lives in the cave and keeps a fire burning in it, will be integrated with tactile and rhythmic experiences of drawing 'C' in sand and in the air, or dancing its shape. At this stage the alphabet letters are represented as nouns and the vowels are usually shown as stars with their own gestures to accompany them. This literacy approach is always a progression from the whole to the parts and integrates sight, sound and movement.

Reading is prepared for in the kindergarten years by the establishment of all the oral and aural skills outlined above; by nurturing a love of literature and the patterned language of story, rhyme and poetry; by promoting and enriching children's narrative abilities; and by respecting and 'reading' children's pictures, gestures, movements and play so that an understanding of signs and symbols is developed. After kindergarten the children in Steiner Waldorf schools begin learning to read by using material they have themselves thought about, talked about and watched their teachers write, and only later move on to strategies for identifying unfamiliar material and using graded reading books.

In all their approaches to literacy, Steiner Waldorf educators are keenly aware of the long historical and cultural background to the human development of writing systems and do not rush children into using abstract symbols that are divorced from context and meaning. Their watchwords might fairly be summed up as 'better late than early' (Moore and Moore 1975). The unpressured context for literacy that is created allows children to explore systems of writing and other signs at their own pace; for example, a 'nearly' 4-year-old made some bold alphabet letters (see Figure 5.11).

At 5 years 6 months, Nicholas could explain his own complex work (see Figure 5.12) to the nursery assistant: this is a calendar. 'This one is today [points to one number "9"]. The drawing is a snowman and the person who made the snowman [drawn below the calendar]'. There are fascinating achievements in this example: Nicholas can write his name and

Figure 5.11 Bold alphabet letters by a 'nearly' 4-year-old.

he is getting to grips with the conventions of calendars, the recording of time and the writing of numerals. Perhaps the snowman drawing is also a reflection of the many illustrated calendars that people now use in homes, offices, shops and schools.

Records and assessment

Steiner Waldorf kindergarten teachers keep records of children's development and evaluate their progress. This includes distinctively 'Steiner' assessments of physical development, music, drawing and cognition/thinking, sometimes in line with the Foundation Stage profile. The Rosebridge Kindergarten in Cambridge provides leaving reports that go with the children if they move on to state or private statutory schooling or to the class teacher at the Cambridge Steiner School and this is accompanied by a statement on 'The Five Year Old Steiner Waldorf Child' (see Appendix III). The teachers meet weekly to discuss the progress of individual children and share their observations and insights. Individual case studies are documented and information is regularly shared with parents.

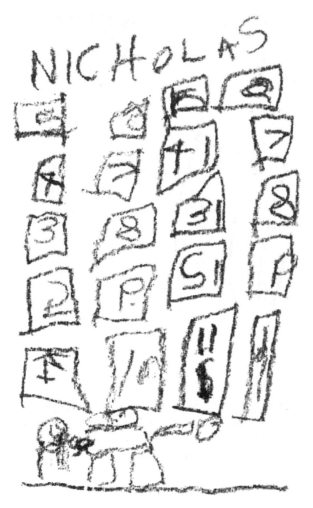

Figure 5.12 Nicholas' calendar.

Earlham Early Years Centre

The setting

Earlham Early Years Centre is located on a pre-Second World War housing estate on the outskirts of Norwich and was purpose-built as a nursery school in an era that emphasized fresh air, outdoor play and cleanliness in early child care and education. The original three classroom building has now been modernized and extended to include a toddler room for 18- to 36-month-olds, a dining room, community rooms and facilities, a sensory room, a ball pool and several consultation rooms and offices. The

Figure 5.13 In the garden.

outdoor space has also been greatly extended and developed and this large garden now features wildlife areas, a hill and shrubberies, a big pond and a shallow rivulet, a grass amphitheatre and a large sand pit with a 'waterfall', a living willow pergola, sensory garden, hard surfaces and plots for digging and growing flowers, fruit and vegetables (Figure 5.13). All the children's rooms open out onto the garden and most curriculum activities take place outside as well as inside. The Centre has a policy of continuous provision (all materials and tools are available to the children all day) and free movement of children between inside and outside spaces for the greater part of the day. The Centre caters for an extended day and year and also provides support and facilities for mother and baby groups, local childminders, community liaison workers and 'stay and play' sessions.

A dispositional curriculum

Since 1999 the staff and the community of Earlham have rejected targets and check lists of skills for children coming to the end of their time in nursery. The shared philosophy of care and education is focused on:

- being rooted in the strengths and challenges of the local community;
- valuing children's abilities and learning strategies;

- acknowledging individual achievements;
- reflecting and respecting the holistic way in which young children learn;
- engaging children and adults in meaningful experiences.

After careful research into several other curriculum models the staff focused on Lilian Katz's work on *learning dispositions* (1995), the Te Whaariki New Zealand curriculum (Carr and May 2000) and the extended work on learning dispositions by Margaret Carr (2001). A disposition is a tendency to show frequently, consciously and voluntarily a pattern of behaviour that is directed to a broad goal. Dispositions include such positive attitudes as curiosity, persistence and cooperation and the documentation for the Foundation Stage in England frequently refers to the importance of children's positive attitudes and dispositions towards learning. The Earlham staff eventually settled on five dispositions that relate to the strengths and needs of their local community:

- Curiosity.
- Persistence.
- Cooperation.
- Rich and flexible communication.
- Playfulness.

Each of these dispositions is defined in terms of:

- what this means for children's learning;
- how the adult can support this learning.

The dispositions are the basis for observations of children and monitoring their progress, medium-term curriculum planning and the implementation of the Foundation Stage curriculum. Each disposition has up to 10 elements that support short-term planning and the close monitoring of the curriculum.

Central to this approach has been the sharing of professional understanding about dispositions with parents and new staff members. Parents have been involved from the start and attend informal sessions in which they share their knowledge of their own children and participate in unpacking the specialist language that professional carers and educators use about individual children's learning dispositions. Several small-scale research projects have supported the dispositional curriculum at Earlham, while in-service training regularly focuses on how dispositions link with child observations and the early learning goals. Video material illustrating what staff are looking for in children's learning and how adults can support this has been recorded at the Centre and is a valuable resource. The Earlham educators are also supported in their ongoing development of the curriculum and their own practice by a 'critical friend'. This is an academic with expertise in the areas of language development and early childhood care and education who gives a wider professional perspective on important issues, leads some in-service training with staff and parents, observes practice and provides feedback.

Rich and flexible in communication

The language and literacy curriculum at Earlham is rooted in the desire to clarify, value and nurture the many ways in which people, children as well as adults, communicate. It also reflects a strong local non-verbal culture.

The elements of the rich and flexible communication disposition illustrate what this means in terms of children's learning. They range from children immersing themselves in sensory experiences (Figure 5.14), observing and imitating others, listening and responding, and going on to explore many other forms of communication and using their bodies to express emotions, ideas and thinking.

There is a group of elements that focus on children using their voices and bodies to communicate their needs and express their individual thoughts and activities. The disposition also encompasses a growing awareness of

Figure 5.14 Immersed in sensory experiences.

Figure 5.15 Using symbols and images.

symbols and images (Figure 5.15); the drive to explore and represent ideas and feelings through symbolic and imaginative play (Figure 5.16); and sharing and communicating their own unique culture.

The adult's role in encouraging children's positive learning disposition towards rich and flexible communication includes modelling, encouragement, responsiveness and tuning in to children's communication strategies. As well as modelling shared pleasure, interest and conversational exchanges, the adult must model being a confident reader, writer, dancer, artist, musician and actor. A general summary of the adult role in supporting the dispositions is included in Appendix IV.

Communication, language and literacy policy

The aims of this policy for communication, language and literacy are:

- to develop and support the skills children need to formulate and express their thoughts, needs and feelings;
- to encourage children to use communicative strategies to assert their individual identity, build self-esteem, initiate and enhance relationships, make sense of the world and get things done.

Figure 5.16 Symbolic and imaginative play.

These aims are achieved by first acknowledging and respecting the languages and communicative strategies that children bring from home and then providing a rich and varied oral and literate environment and thoughtful, responsive adults to share it with (see Appendix IV).

Summary: the essence of the case studies

The introduction to this chapter suggested that case studies can capture the essence of a human situation or institution, but these particular studies also offer alternative perspectives on early years practice. This is of considerable importance in a period of increasingly narrow definitions of childhood, learning, curriculum and literacy and the related regulations for early and statutory schooling. The following comments attempt to pin down what is shared by, and central to, these unique early years settings.

They are strongly focused on child development and affirm that the first duty of early years educators is to tune in to children, have faith in their powers as thinkers and social beings and by implication, understand what they are observing and know how to support and extend their potential.

This approach is supported by research into the qualities and abilities of successful early years educators (Blenkin and Kelly 1997; Siraj-Blatchford et al. 2002; Sylva et al. 2004; Moyles 2007).

All the settings have a strong commitment to protecting and nurturing childhood and children's opportunities for play and symbolic representation of many kinds. This is based on a professional understanding that children's self-esteem and thinking is rooted in play and representation. It also reflects a crucial insight about literacy: that it is one of many symbolic systems for representing thinking and experience, so that puppets and stories, role play and block constructions, for example, can support the processes of writing and reading.

These settings promote a rich oral (talking) and aural (listening) curriculum and a literary approach based on stories, rhyme and poetry. They do so because they know that the combination of spoken language, gossip and discussion, and patterned literary language provides a direct bridge to literacy. This oracy curriculum could be the basic 'basic' that makes all the difference in the early years.

Despite some distinctive differences around the issue of direct literacy instruction, all the case study settings are agreed on the need for early literacy to be encountered in meaningful contexts that relate directly to human purposes, interests and needs.

The role of the early years educator and carer is seen in essentially similar ways in these settings. Direct telling and instructing is less important or useful than engaging in shared learning alongside children so that joint meanings can be created. In this sense children's thinking and learning is 'scaffolded' and the adults are models of what it means to be talkers, thinkers, doers and imaginers.

The final and perhaps most urgent of all the themes to emerge from these case studies concerns the issue of imposing formal and so-called academic instruction on young children. There is growing contemporary evidence to add to the long-established view that early formal teaching damages young children's potential for creative thinking, undermines their self-esteem and social confidence, and may well turn them off from the later years of schooling. This issue is central to the discussion of the national frameworks for language that follows in Chapter 6.

Note

1 The first two paragraphs in this section draw on material in *Steiner Waldorf Education: Aims, Methods and Curriculum*, edited by M. Rawson (1997). Sally Jenkinson, author of *The Genius of Play* (2001) and former Early Years Adviser, Steiner Education, UK, compiled and wrote the remaining material.

Further reading

Edgington, M. (2004) *The Foundation Stage Teacher in Action: Teaching 3, 4 and 5 Year Olds*, 3rd edn. London: Paul Chapman.

Nicol, J. (2007) *Bringing the Steiner Waldorf Approach to Your Early Years Practice*. Abingdon: Routledge.

Thornton, L. and Brunton, P. (2007) *Bringing the Reggio Approach to Your Early Years Practice*. Abingdon: Routledge.

National requirements for language and literacy in the early years

> I arrived at the prison with 14 other inmates, all of whom had just been found guilty of breaking the rules of grammar. Ever since people started being a bit tougher with how they imposed education standards, more and more of us were put in the slammer.
>
> (Iannucci 1998)

This chapter focuses on:

- a brief overview of national statutes and guidelines for early years curricula in England, Wales, Scotland and Northern Ireland;
- a case study from a Foundation Stage class in an infant school;
- the dangers of early formal education;
- four essential strategies for language and literacy learning.

Note: An official website address is given for each country or region of the UK as the frameworks are often changed and some proposals are still out for consultation.

Changes, changes . . . National statutes and guidance

From birth, children in England who receive care and education outside the home are now directly affected by education and care legislation and advisory frameworks. Similar interventions are also impacting very young children and their families in Wales, Scotland and Northern Ireland. These different requirements and changes in the UK come thick and fast, making it difficult to evaluate their impact or monitor their quality. However, there is no escaping the fact that the learning and teaching of communication, language and literacy in early years settings and schools are shaped by this constant flurry of orders and guidance. Furthermore, the effect these frequent changes have on the views and understandings of families, carers and professional practitioners is complex and difficult to assess. We all need to know about the national requirements that we live with, but, more importantly, we need to respond to them in the context of our knowledge of child development, language and literacy development and broad international approaches to early care and education. The main focus of this review will be on the situation in England because of its influence across the UK and because it is an interesting example of strong control by government of curriculum and practice.

England – from Early Years Foundation Stage to Primary Frameworks

The Statutory Framework for the Early Years Foundation Stage (EYFS) became mandatory for all early years providers and schools in September 2008 and applies to children from birth to five in all OfSTED (Office for Standards in Education) registered settings. The EYFS builds on previous legislation and guidance, in particular, the Curriculum Guidance for the Foundation Stage (DfES/QCA 2000) and the Birth to Three Matters project and framework (DfES/Sure Start 2002). These influences permeate the new framework to some extent and provide the themes for its principled approach with regard to:

- A Unique Child;
- Positive Relationships;
- Enabling Environments;
- Learning and Development.

This approach highlights the importance of focusing on children as unique individuals, supporting their relationships and learning in companionship, following their learning and development stories and emphasizing the significance of play in all aspects of development. There is a useful 'shorthand' term that can be used to characterize this approach and that is 'holistic'. It is both a philosophical stance and a theoretical basis for practice and informs the previous chapters of this book. However, the specific learning and development requirements of the framework are problematic because they still reflect the traditional school-based outcomes objectives of the earlier Foundation Stage document (2000). They are difficult to relate to work with under-3s because they are often worryingly inappropriate for infants and toddlers.

There are six areas of early learning goals with their associated education programmes:

- Personal, Social and Emotional Development;
- Communication, Language and Literacy;
- Problem Solving, Reasoning and Numeracy;
- Knowledge and Understanding of the World;
- Physical Development;
- Creative Development.

Communication, language and literacy

It is encouraging to see that communication is recognized as being at the centre of language and literacy development, but the 19 early learning goals to be achieved by the end of the EYFS (age 5) are quite a mixed bunch! They do include such sensible aims as enjoying and responding to spoken and written language, stories, songs, rhymes, poems and music. Also included are understanding how narratives and stories work, extending vocabulary, knowing about the conventions of print in English and beginning to write for different purposes.

There is, however, another agenda being imposed on the EYFS framework and this is revealed by some unrealistic and inappropriate goals relating to early reading. What is now officially called 'the simple view of reading', with its exclusive reliance on systematic, synthetic phonics, is reflected in the requirements that children should:

- hear and say sounds in words in the order in which they occur;
- link sounds to letters, naming and sounding the letters of the alphabet;
- use their phonic knowledge to write simple regular words and make phonetically plausible attempts at more complex words;
- write their own names and other things such as labels and captions, and begin to form simple sentences, sometimes using punctuation.

These latter two goals have been critic   by linguists and
early years specialists in the UK as be   act, arbitrary and
developmentally inappropriate for all 5-year-olds to achieve. Currently, it
has been confirmed that these two goals are to be 'reviewed' by the author of
the Rose Report (DfES 2006). It is possible that aspects of these requirements
could be tackled by some children in playful situations with sensitive and
trained adults and the case study later in this chapter offers some examples
of 5-year-olds using their developing phonic knowledge with great flair
and creativity! But, these goals could also be a recipe for literacy disaster if
imposed willy-nilly on all children who are under 5 years old and we need
to remember that most children in the UK are already in Reception classes
at the age of 4. These 'goals' should certainly be postponed until at least
the end of Key Stage 1 (age 7), in line with the practices of many countries
with far higher levels of national literacy.

Letters and Sounds (DfES 2007b)

This document, which sets out to describe the 'Principles and Practice
of High Quality Phonics', has the status of 'guidance' for primary
practitioners. Although it is not mandatory, it describes in some detail
a six-phase teaching programme. It is, therefore, difficult to avoid the
conclusion that this is how the synthetic phonics recommendations of
the Rose Review are expected to be implemented in early years and
primary classrooms. Even more disturbing for early years practitioners
and providers is the fact that the programme reaches down into the
EYFS, although it runs counter to the spirit of the core principles in that
framework. For example, what of the learning story of each unique child
who has highly individual experiences, starting points and dispositions
for learning? Similarly, the significance of play as an activity chosen
by children and driven by personal needs, passions and investigations,
bears no relationship to the kind of 'playing with sounds' described in
this strictly regulated phonics programme. The emphasis in the EYFS
documentation is on young children learning and developing in close
relationships with significant others, adults and peers, and finding mutual
delight in shared meaning and understanding. This approach does not
sit easily alongside the imposition of inappropriate, meaningless word
'games'.

We have, of course, been here before with the daily Literacy Hour that
was also 'advisory', but still became difficult to avoid. It too is tightly
structured and features timed elements of instruction and activity (DfEE

1998). The current requirements for daily phonics sessions in Reception and Key Stage 1 classes (5–7 years) fit neatly into the pattern set by the Literacy Hour. In fact, there are some indications that the daily phonics lessons will supersede the Literacy Hour as the new Primary Framework for Literacy becomes established.

The Primary Framework for Literacy starts with the Early Learning Goals for Communication, Language and Literacy at the end of the Foundation Stage and then builds on to this base a complex structure of 'Aspects' and 'Strands'.

The six Aspects of the Literacy Framework

- Handwriting.
- Language for communicating.
- Language for thinking.
- Linking sounds and letters.
- Reading.
- Writing.

The 12 Strands of the framework are broken down into year-by-year objectives for the whole of the primary phase of schooling (5–11 years).

The 12 Strands of Literacy

- Speaking.
- Listening and responding.
- Group discussion and instruction.
- Drama.
- Word recognition.
- Word structure and spelling.
- Understand and interpret texts.
- Engage with and respond to texts.
- Creating and shaping texts.
- Text structure and organization.
- Sentence structure and punctuation.
- Presentation.

Early Reading in the primary years is defined as a word recognition task, thus early reading is decoding and this is the 'simple view of reading'!

Perhaps the essence of this is best encapsulated in the Strand 5 (word recognition) Foundation Stage objective:

Read simple words by sounding out and blending the phonemes all through the word from left to right

Note: Children move from reading simple consonant-vowel-consonant (CVC) words such as 'cat' and 'bus' to longer CCVC words such as 'clap' and 'stop', and CVCC words as 'fast' and 'milk'

I believe that it was in order to subvert instructional material like this that Dr Seuss introduced the 'Cat in the Hat' to the English-speaking world! So, because this is the English language that is being decoded, the end of Year 1 (5–6 years) objectives pile on the confusion for our phonically well-drilled children as they are told that the graphemes and phonemes they have learnt can actually be spelt in many different ways!

- The grapheme 'g' is pronounced differently in 'get' and 'gem'.
- The grapheme 'ow' is pronounced differently in 'how' and 'show'.
- The /ae/ sound can be spelt with 'ai', 'ay' or 'ae'.
- The /ee/ sound can also be spelt as 'ea' and 'e'.

However, when the frameworks are not dealing with reading they can be helpful and supportive; for example, 'Listening and responding' and 'Creating and shaping texts' offer useful aims for Foundation Stage and Year 1 educators and children.

Note: Further information can be accessed at www.standards.dcsf.gov.uk/primaryframeworks.

Wales – the learning country

Ever since devolution in 1999 Wales has wished to be known as 'the learning country' and, significantly for this discussion, Wales is the only officially bilingual country in the UK although small numbers of Gaelic speakers can be found in Scotland and Northern Ireland. The Welsh Foundation Phase (FP) is currently being introduced for all children aged 3–5 in the period September 2008 to July 2010 and extended to 6- and 7-year-olds in 2011 and 2012. In the new FP curriculum 'Welsh Language and

Development' is a subject in its own right, alongside 'Language, Literacy and Communication'. The Welsh language has been a compulsory subject in schools since 1990, either as a first language in Welsh-medium schools, or as a second language in English-medium settings. Welsh-medium schools use the immersion strategy for developing Welsh language skills but the FP in English-medium schools will provide many opportunities for children to learn and enjoy using the Welsh language through daily Welsh-medium play-based activities. The FP for all children in Wales approaches early literacy by creating a firm base in speaking and listening skills and encouraging children to talk about their own feelings and experiences.

The distinctive quality of care and education in Wales is not simply a matter of bilingualism, but arises from a philosophy that reflects an interest in well-established international practices. Children are seen as creative, independent and physically active learners and the FP curriculum promotes outdoor play and investigation. There are no national tests and league tables in the primary years and teacher observations and assessments are the means of monitoring children's progress and planning for development.

Families with children under 3 years old have some opportunities to access Welsh-medium daycare and nursery settings alongside English-medium provision. These settings are provided by the usual mix of government initiatives, charities and private 'for profit' organizations and their distribution is uneven in rural areas, remote villages and the poorer neighbourhoods in towns and cities. The government Flying Start programme (2005) aims to integrate childcare, early learning, parenting and health services for families with under-3s. This initiative is focused on eradicating child poverty and the inequalities of provision and opportunity across the principality and includes a focus on literacy and 'books for babies'.

Note: Further information can be accessed at www.learning.wales.gov.uk.

Scotland

Scotland has always enjoyed independent control over its own education system and the Scottish Parliament continues to develop legislation for care and education from birth to 18 years of age.

Devolution has given considerable impetus to the ongoing debate about education and new approaches to family welfare, care, education and the curriculum are currently out for consultation, or about to be implemented.

Birth to Three: Supporting our Youngest Children (2005) identifies three key factors in good practice:

- Relationships;
- Responsive care;
- Respect.

These 'three Rs' reflect an awareness of the significance of initial attachments in a child's life and this is the underlying theme of the guidance. The document also highlights the importance of 'tuning in' to very young children and 'keeping them in mind'. A final section on 'Reflections' begins with a direct quotation from a popular picture book – what a radical breakthrough for a government policy document!

> *'My babies know I will look after them ... I'm their mum.' 'How do you look after them?' Mum asked, and Rosie said 'I make them their teas and I tell them stories and I take them for walks and I talk to them and I tell them that I love them.'*
>
> (Waddell 1990)

The current *Curriculum Framework for Children 3–5* has five areas and children's progress is assessed by teachers:

- Emotional, Personal and Social Development;
- Knowledge and Understanding of the World;
- Communication and Language;
- Expressive and Aesthetic Development;
- Physical Development and Movement.

Similar curriculum areas are featured in the existing *5–14 Curriculum Guidelines* and teacher assessments are used to monitor children's progress:

- Personal and Social Development;
- Religious and Moral Education;
- Environmental Studies;
- Mathematics;
- Language (plus a modern language);
- Expressive Arts.

However, these two curriculum phases are about to be subsumed into the new *Curriculum for Excellence 3–18* (2008/09), which will emphasize smooth transitions between age-related phases of care and education, extending pre-school approaches into primary schooling and creating opportunities for play and investigation in school.

The latest project out for consultation in Scotland is *Early Years and Early Intervention* and it focuses on the period from pre-conception and pregnancy, through birth and up to age 8. This is an ambitious remit but the policy is driven by the belief that early intervention and getting it right in the early years is effective and has the potential to transform lives. There is considerable emphasis on integrated early years services, supporting families with young children, managing effective transitions in education, equipping children with good literacy and numeracy skills and achieving small classes in the early primary years. There is also a reference to 'securing the place of Gaelic within early years services'.

Note: Further information can be accessed at www.scotland.gov.uk/ publications.

Northern Ireland

Early years care and education in Northern Ireland is strongly influenced by some features that are unique to the province. First, young children must start formal compulsory schooling in the year they become 5 years old, regardless of how very close to 4 years old they may be (for this purpose the start of the school year is 1 July). There is currently only one intake of children in September. Second, the 11+ examination taken at the end of Key Stage 2 exerts another pressure for formal learning on the early years, the new Foundation Stage and Key Stages 1 and 2 (6–8 years and 8–11 years). This examination decides whether children will transfer to a grammar school or a secondary school. Third, because of the complex political and religious history of Northern Ireland, schooling is still predominantly segregated along religious lines and primary schools tend to serve either a catholic or a protestant local community.

There is no framework of guidance for children under 3 years old. The revised *Curricular Guidance for Pre-school Education* (2006) applies to 3–4-year-olds and reflects a child-centred approach and emphasizes play and enjoyment in early learning, as well as equal opportunities for all children so that they feel valued and secure.

In schools some Primary 1 and 2 classes have been working with an 'enriched curriculum' in which a play-based and active approach to learning is used for parts of the day, but children still have lessons in shared reading, phonological awareness, shared writing and mathematics. This pilot has now influenced the introduction of a Foundation Stage as part of the *Revised Northern Ireland Curriculum* (2006) and since September 2007 the years Primary 1 and 2 have become the new Foundation Stage. Language and literacy is one of the six areas of learning in the primary curriculum (plus religious education) but in the new Foundation Stage there will be a greater emphasis on oral language and emergent literacy activities.

Areas of learning in the Revised Primary Curriculum

- Language and Literacy.
- Mathematics and Numeracy.
- The Arts.
- The World Around Us.
- Personal Development and Mutual Understanding.
- Physical Education.
- Religious education.

Note: Further information can be accessed from www.deni.gov.uk.

The one common element in this picture of differing UK practices is the presence of 4-year-old children in settings dominated by traditional curricular guidelines and goals and the downward pressure of a formal primary curriculum. In other countries 4-year-olds would start their formal schooling at a much later stage and their pre-school settings would be free to concentrate on the basics of learning to learn, emotional well-being and self-esteem and social and cultural development. However, even within the tight parameters of the last year of the English Foundation Stage, some outstanding practitioners can still implement an inspirational and developmentally appropriate curriculum.

The Foundation Stage in an infant school

Case study by class teachers Mary Fisher and Shelagh Swallow

St John's Roman Catholic Infant School caters for 180 children aged 4–7 years and serves the Catholic community in Norwich and the surrounding area. The school Foundation Stage consists of one large open-plan classroom, with a team of two teachers, two classroom assistants and 60 children. At present the school does not have any pre-school provision, so the children starting school come from many different settings.

Every September 60 children are welcomed into their new classroom at St John's. They engage in a play-based, emergent curriculum through which children are encouraged to be self-regulating, active learners. As early years practitioners we are aware of the importance of:

- achieving a high level of well-being in order for children to be able to access their learning;
- nurturing children's positive dispositions;
- creating an environment where children are encouraged to explore and express their own ideas, knowing that they are valued;
- providing valuable, purposeful and, above all, enjoyable learning experiences appropriate to the child's stage of development.

Talking and Listening

Talking is a key aspect of our learning environment – it is in everything we do. When the children arrive in the classroom every morning we greet them individually by name. We always build in an informal 'conversation time' in which the children sit and chat socially on the carpet before register time. We have adapted register time, from what was traditionally an adult-led activity, to a child-led activity. The idea works well as it builds on the natural interest that the children have in each other and each others' names. Together with the children we have devised a visual register of the class. The children can use a variety of strategies to take the register; for example, the pictures, names and numbers on the register correspond to our class number line where the children's photos, together with their numbers and names, are prominently displayed. The children take turns to call the register and they are encouraged to record absences and attendances using their own emergent marks. Finally, they return their register to the school secretary and articulate the information they have gathered to her. The children are always anxious to explain their data clearly as they are motivated by their acute understanding of the consequences of getting the dinner numbers wrong. Food is central to their world! This whole process enables them to take responsibility and to communicate for a real purpose.

We have moved away from a carpet session as a didactic teacher-led time, where the practitioner talks and the children are expected to listen, into times where the children are empowered to be leaders and facilitators of their own learning. We use carpet times to develop their thinking skills. We scaffold the sessions to enable the children to formulate and share their ideas with the group and we constantly encourage the children to make links with their previous learning. For example, we have recognized the potential of 'show and tell' as a vehicle for developing children's lateral thinking skills. Children are encouraged to bring in objects for 'show and tell' but we stipulate that the object must relate, in some way, to our current topic. We have recently been using Turner's 'Fighting Temeraire' painting as a catalyst for our learning. Ben brought in an orange toy worm. The children asked various questions to try and ascertain the link that Ben had in mind between his worm and the Temeraire. Thomas said, 'Did a seagull drop it on board as it flew over?' 'No', Ben replied and after a while he told us that it was a woodworm that was munching its way through the wooden floorboards of the ship. The next day Ben brought a similar green worm to school and we all thought it was another woodworm, but Ben had a different thought about his worm. 'Did the sailors use it to try and catch a fish?' Lily asked. But Ben said 'No' and, after a series of unsuccessful guesses, he told us that the sailors might have had a bowl of fruit on board and maybe there was an apple in the bowl and this worm crawled out of the apple! The children listened carefully to Ben and were intrigued by his explanation. Later that day, William found an acorn with a tiny round hole in it and immediately made a connection with Ben's worm, highlighting the power of philosophical thought and the child's role as a facilitator.

We provide opportunities for developing the skill of asking questions by using a 'feely bag' containing a mystery object chosen by one child about which the other children ask 'thinking questions'. This exercise requires all the children to listen to each other's questions and the answers, in order to modify their own questions and build up a bank of clues as to the identity of the hidden object. After many questions have been asked one child is selected to feel inside the bag and hopefully identify the contents, thus winning the chance to take the feely bag home and lead the game the following day. As the children become familiar with the process their questions become more thoughtful and deductive. The children also become more adventurous in the objects they select for the bag. Amy chose a tea-bag, Travis chose a coat hanger and Emily, whose Dad is a plumber, chose a tap as the mystery object. Questions evolved such as, 'Do you use it in the kitchen? Is it made of plastic? Can you twist it?'

We extend the children's questioning skills by using clip boards and making it a job on the daily job-board of independent tasks that the children are expected to complete. The 'clipboard job' requires children to move around the busy classroom asking an agreed question and recording the answers that are given in their own emergent way.

This is a rich learning opportunity involving speaking, listening, writing and reading back data. When we had class chickens we formulated many interesting questions to ask such as: 'Why do chickens have feathers?' (Figure 6.1) and 'Do chickens have nostrils?' (Figure 6.2).

Figure 6.1 Why do chickens have feathers?

The children are highly motivated in this type of task as they have formulated the questions and they want to compare their findings with their peers. We display their recordings prominently to document our work for parents and others to see, but also so that the children can see that we value their recording and that it conveys important information to others.

We use gathering times to sing our own songs and rhymes using phonics and alliteration for all kinds of purposes; for example, we have made up a 'fix it' song to the tune of 'Bob the Builder' to help us solve each other's problems and a 'tidy up' song. At fruit time we make up rhymes and alliterations about the fruit: did you ever see a bear eat a pear? Did you ever eat a peach on the beach? This has given the children the confidence to experiment with sounds, word building, storytelling and rhyme making (Figures 6.3 and 6.4) and we have heard them making up their own songs in the writing corner and while riding the trikes in the outside area.

Figure 6.2 Do chickens have nostrils?

Figure 6.3 Experiments with words, storytelling and rhyme making.

Figure 6.4 Experiments with words, storytelling and rhyme making.

Planning

We plan in a flexible, open-ended way so that the children's ideas are valued and may determine the direction for subsequent learning. As early years practitioners we have sound knowledge of the curriculum aims and objectives but recognize that these are most effectively achieved when the children are engaged in tasks that have meaning for them. When children see that not only do we listen to their ideas, but they can also impact on our learning and change its direction, they are encouraged even more to express themselves knowing that their ideas are valued. They also begin to appreciate that they can learn from each other. We record this type of planning in a mind map form that we share with the children and the parents in a display. Mind maps encourage the children to make connections with previous learning and to link new ideas in a cross-curricular way. We can add to them continually so they reflect the fluidity of our

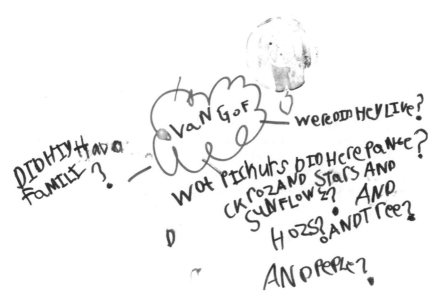

Figure 6.5 Questions about Van Gogh.

approach. George made his own mind map of questions he would like to ask about Van Gogh (Figure 6.5). All the children's recording is displayed and documented to explain their learning journeys and to inform future planning.

One of our topics was inspired by Van Gogh's painting 'Starry Night'. We looked at this painting and it led to all kinds of work about the stars, the dark, space, and so on. After noticing the houses in the town a child wondered, 'Was there a mouse in the house?' That question took our learning in a whole new direction! This child-initiated idea led us to investigate cheese, holes, mice, windmills (from the song 'A mouse lived in a windmill ...') flour, recipes and many more things. After a lot of work we decided to gather our ideas together in a celebration and like all great parties, food was at the centre. Preparations involved the children making mouse costumes with paper ears, tails and bow-ties. They also made mice-themed food – mainly cheese-flavoured! We had a treasure hunt, played a variety of mice-related games, sang songs and had a great deal of fun. The preparations involved much discussion, negotiating, listening to each other and agreeing a plan of action. The celebration itself was cross-curricular and catered for all learning styles. We regularly celebrate a topic with a party and find it makes a very effective plenary!

Stories and storytelling

In a classroom where talking is valued there are many opportunities for storytelling. We listen to the children recounting their news and help them to sequence events. This is the beginning of storytelling. We recognize the wealth of opportunities for sequencing and storytelling that a rich learning environment can offer, for example, following recipes and perhaps writing their own imaginary ones: a recipe for a happy fish; following instructions to plant a seed; mix paint or make bubble mixture. We write instructions using pictures and words and encourage the children to communicate their own instructions in the same way. This demonstrates to the children how to use word and picture cues for reading. In our many role-play scenarios the children physically follow the sequence of a story in which they are the central characters. To go on a holiday to a hot or cold country, for example, they first have to select their preferred destination at the travel shop, book a ticket and then be vaccinated appropriately at the health centre. From there they go to the holiday shop to buy suitable clothes and then to the airport, to passport control, baggage control, the boarding lounge and onto the plane that takes them finally to their destination. This role-play sequence offers many opportunities for mini-stories to be told and acted out on the way; for instance, the story of the bag that is too heavy to be accepted by baggage control, or the lost passport. Role play is a fantastic vehicle for children to become engaged in high-level learning using all their sense to relate to one another and solve problems in real-life scenarios.

Emergent writing and reading

There are signs all around our classroom that convey important messages to all of us. We handwrite all our notices and display the children's emergent writing alongside our own. We encourage the children to make their own signs and notices and they are particularly keen to write 'NO' signs when something is out of order or if bad weather means that we cannot go outside. They make signs for the role play with messages such as, 'No dogs allowed', or 'Listen for your flight!' and accompany their marks with a picture.

The 'Writing Corner' is a very prominent area of the classroom and loved by most of the children. We supply all kinds of writing material including glitter pens, light-up pens, felt tips, gel pens, paper, envelopes, and so on. All the children are treated as writers from the beginning and this is reflected in our displays. We model writing and scribe the children's stories and comments. We work with the children in small groups enabling them to apply their developing phonic knowledge to their emergent writing. Through our many role-play scenarios and independent activities the children are required to write for a variety of purposes.

Another important feature of our class is the library. The books are categorized by a colour code into fiction and non-fiction. The children have specific days to change their shared reading books to take home. They are taught how to operate this system independently with two children at a time taking it in turn to be the librarians. They have a list of children to bring to the library and a logbook to fill in for books returned. This builds on the interest that children have in each other's names, encouraging them to be able to read these names using a variety of cues. We have regular visitors to our library who read to the children in small groups and individually. We encourage grandparents and retired friends of the school to take on this role. Children are encouraged to be readers right from the start by storytelling, role play, taking the register, running the library, following recipes and instructions and sharing books at home and at school, as a class, in small groups or individually.

Early bloomers and late frosts

In contrast to this account of a dynamic and truly learner-centred class, the kind of early years practice we are in danger of being hurried into by current legislation reflects the following misunderstandings:

- young children learn by sitting for lengthy periods of time and listening to instructions;
- the labelling of written language forms and features and the drilling of letter sounds enables children to write and read effectively;
- doing more of the same drills at home every night will ensure children's educational progress;
- children's feelings, dispositions, social experiences and some control over how and when they learn have no place in education;
- teaching is merely a matter of telling;
- once targets have been identified, learning takes place in simple, incremental stages.

There is, however, a long tradition of gardening metaphors in early years education in Europe: the kindergarten is a garden of children and the healthy mind and body were thought to be essential to learning, so the early pioneers created open-air classrooms in gardens and on verandahs. Many of these nursery educators rescued the children they taught from poverty, semi-starvation, criminal neglect and exploitation in the slums of towns and cities, and it is helpful to remember that a 'nursery' is also a place where young plants are nurtured! So, as we still talk of nurturing children and watching them blossom into confident young people, it is not unreasonable to remind ourselves that young blooms that are forced on too soon are often weak and likely to be struck down by a late frost.

These issues of 'too much too soon', or 'better late than early' were referred to in the previous chapter and are at the heart of the Steiner Waldorf UK Kindergartens' reservations about some of the recent curriculum legislation. There is research evidence that, in the long term, a very early start to formal education damages children's social and intellectual development (Nabuco and Sylva 1996; Nutbrown 1998; Meyer 2002; Altwerger 2005). Add to this the facts that most European countries start formal schooling much later than the UK but have a comprehensive system of pre-school care and education and excellent rates of adult literacy and numeracy, as well as enviable skills as speakers of two or more languages. The curriculum in the European kindergartens avoids the early written recording of mathematics, the introduction of reading scheme books and the copying of letters and sentences because of evidence that early recording of this kind actually gets in the way of young children's understanding and thinking. The emphasis is on play and an oral curriculum which emphasizes:

- talking;
- listening;
- discussions;
- storytelling;
- rhyme and poetry;
- play with the sounds of language (alliteration and rhyme again);
- drama;
- music;
- painting and drawing;
- modelling and gardening;
- group activities and the careful development of children's self-esteem and creativity;
- learning outdoors in gardens, forests and public spaces.

Rigorous long-term research in the USA and the UK has shown that the advantages of a high-quality informal nursery education persist into adulthood and save a society both the expense and the human waste and misery of much youth crime, truancy, drug addiction and teenage pregnancies (Ball 1994; Schweinhart and Weikart 1997). A further strengthening of this evidence was provided by an American study on the long-term advantages of an early years and primary curriculum that emphasized literature and the arts (Heath 1997). Children at the start of this study (40 years ago) were more likely to have had a primary education that was arts-based, yet these children who read more literature and did more drawing also did more writing. They did more writing in fact than their own children who had been drawn into narrower and more basic 'three Rs' approaches in recent years. The original children from the early period of the study also proved to be more creative and flexible and happier with mathematics, science and complex ideas. The study is continuing to look at adolescents from low-income, multilingual, multicultural urban backgrounds who voluntarily involve themselves in independent theatre and dance groups and interesting findings emerge. These young people stay on longer in education, have strong self-esteem and independence, win awards for achievement and good attendance at secondary school, involve themselves in community service and enjoy maths and science. This research seems to indicate that there is an individual bonus of self-esteem associated with an early 'arts and humanities' start to life and schooling, perhaps because prolonged exposure to stories and literature helps children to think in a hypothetical, or 'what if' mode, and not be afraid of being tentative or not knowing things.

If good-quality informal nursery education and care protects young children from the late frosts of a disturbed or criminal adolescence and gives them a sense of self-worth and the ability to think independently, we should want it for all our children. But there is also the late frost of alienation from schooling and all things educational that blights much of our secondary school system as well as the lives of many young adults. Evidence that this begins in the very first days and weeks of infant school has been around for a very long time (Barrett 1986; Bennett and Kell 1989; Sherman 1996; Brooker 2002) and it highlights the dangers of lack of individual attention and the failure of teachers to tune in to the abilities and concerns of very young children in their first weeks in school. Current research from the University of Cambridge continues to focus on these concerns and points to the failings of a curriculum that does not allow children to be active, involved, talkative and playful (The Primary Review 2008 – see website address on p. 175). A range of international research into learning to read stresses:

- the need for very careful settling-in procedures in the early days of school;
- lots of individual and small group work with a teacher;

- language and literacy experiences that are pleasurable and meaningful;
- respect for all the literacy learning children bring to school from home (see, Weinberger 1996; Serpell, Baker and Sonnenschein 2005; Riley 2006; Gregory 2008).

Four essential strategies for language and literacy learning

Talk, play and representation

The earlier chapters of this book have given high priority to these aspects of early development and learning: spoken language remains central to the curriculum because it shapes all our thinking, enabling us not simply to communicate with others but understand their thinking too. It is the means by which young children make sense of experiences, information and new knowledge and talk is still one important method for teaching skills and sharing knowledge. Talk, play and representation are symbolic systems and central to the kinds of thinking that distinguish human behaviour and culture. They are all ways of letting words, pictures, gestures, clothes, rituals and many other activities – from gardening to carving totems – stand for, or represent, complex attitudes, beliefs and feelings.

> Literacy depends on these basics: talk, play and representation.

Rhyme, rhythm and language patterns

Previous chapters on play with language have emphasized rhythm, repetition and the patterns of sounds that are usually associated with poetry. These musical qualities of any language are a major help to the young speaker who is making the move from talking to understanding print and its relationships with spoken language. For one thing, these striking and enjoyable aspects of language have the effect of making it very obvious to the child that sounds are repeated again and again, or are similar but not quite the same, or produce a musical rhythm or beat that can be tapped, clapped, stamped, danced to or sung. This makes language very obvious and an object of interest to investigate rather than a taken-for-granted, practical and unremarkable method of communication. Just as fine poetry can stop us in our tracks, so rhymes, alliteration, rhythmic patterns of language, songs, nonsense verse and unusual words grab our attention at any age and can make language study possible and delightful for young children.

> Literacy depends on these basics: rhyme, rhythm and language patterns.

Stories and narrative

Chapter 3 set out the significance of stories and narrative in human thinking and sense-making and their role in helping children to understand particular ways of thinking and using language that are most commonly found in books. Many encounters with told stories, picture books and story books enable children to get a hold on literary language, book language and the nature and conventions of print – including the ways in which we make meanings out of pictures and written narratives. These are important early lessons about how to be a reader.

> Literacy depends on these basics: stories and narratives.

Environmental print and messages

Early lessons about what writing is for, what writers do and how print works have been described in Chapter 4 and in the case study above. The best way to get children started on understanding that print carries messages and is available for all of us to use for our own purposes is to draw children's attention to print in their environment at every opportunity, make collections of it and spend time reading it with them. We can encourage them to play with the print, taking it apart and reassembling it, or making copies of it for their play areas, outdoor spaces, classrooms and homes. We should make a constant practice of writing and drawing messages and signs for our children, as well as helping them to make their own meaningful marks and messages to send to a widening range of audiences.

> Literacy depends on these basics: environmental print and messages.

Summary

Early years care and education in the UK is increasingly subjected to very tight controls that set out not just appropriate health and safety regulations and curriculum content, but even stipulate how these requirements should be 'delivered' by practitioners and teachers. In England the Early Years Foundation Stage curriculum applies to the youngest babies receiving care in settings outside the home, including childminding, daycare and children's centres.

The one province and three countries of the Union have distinctively different approaches and correspondingly different national frameworks and requirements, but they are similar in their very early start to formal schooling. The dangers of 'too much too soon' have been known for many years and children's successful language and literacy development requires a rich and broad approach to play, communication, early symbolizing and mark-making, talking and storying. The case study in this chapter of children in one school at the end of the Foundation Stage provides encouraging evidence that a more active and playful approach to learning, including language and literacy, is not only possible but desirable and hugely rewarding for children and their families.

Further reading

Bruce, T. (ed.) (2006) *Early Childhood*. London: Sage Publications.

Clark, M.M. and Waller, T. (eds) (2007) *Early Childhood Education and Care: Policy and Practice*. London: Sage Publications.

Moyles, J. (ed.) (2007) *Early Years Foundations: Meeting the Challenge*. Maidenhead: Open University Press.

Riley, J. (2006) *Language and Literacy 3–7*. London: Paul Chapman.

Stannard, J. and Huxford, L. (2007) *The Literacy Game: The Story of the National Literacy Strategy*. Abingdon: Routledge.

www.primaryreview.org.uk

7

Communicating and talking together

'And how many hours a day did you do lessons?' said Alice, in a hurry to change the subject.
'Ten hours the first day' said the Mock Turtle: 'nine the next, and so on.'
'What a curious plan!' exclaimed Alice.
'That's the reason they're called lessons,' the Gryphon remarked: 'because they lessen from day to day.'

(Carroll [1865] 1998: 85)

This chapter focuses on:

- children communicating and talking;
- listening to children;
- parents, professional carers and educators;
- finding our voices;
- looking at early years settings;
- last words.

It is only to be expected that a book about language development will end where it began – by returning to the importance for all of us of communicating and talking, especially when, like Alice, we are faced with educational terminology that has not got easier to explain in the years since 1865. So the final sections of this book will focus briefly on children communicating and talking, on listening to children, on parents, professional carers and educators talking, and on the crucial need for all of us to find a voice and make a difference to care and education in the early years.

Children communicating and talking

There is no intention here to repeat all the material in the first chapter of this book, but we must never forget that babies and young children start off as 'great communicators'. Their enormous potential for thinking and communicating is fostered and developed into the ability to speak and understand one or more languages by the simple fact that carers take them seriously, talk to them constantly as they go about the business of daily living and involve them in more and more of their activities and interests. Very young children's potential for talk is nurtured and developed by their adult carers who delight in the children's sociability, curiosity and capacity for fun. These adult carers are themselves continually rewarded and motivated by the responses of the children they live with or work with in some professional capacity. It is important to reassert these positive and optimistic claims about children's huge potential for communicating, talking and thinking and the crucial nurturing roles of the adults who first care for them. The current preoccupation with testing and ranking children, institutions and professionals could create a tendency to think of children as potential failures and problems who might give us trouble and lower our ratings in the scramble for funds, staff or adequate 'numbers'. This is a book which, like the series of books it is part of, celebrates children and their carers and educators and seeks to share the excitement of language development – and all other aspects of child development.

Opportunities to be with other children and play with them, or alongside them, also extend the social and linguistic skills of young children and start them off on the long process of adjusting to the existence and the demands of their peers and of replacing many impulsive physical reactions with words and reasons. This is the business of thinking and mediating, rather than lashing out in blind rage, and it takes us all a long time to get it right – if we ever do! Social play with other children has other very positive linguistic and social advantages – namely, helping children to extend their own experiences, knowledge, communication strategies and language by allowing them to take over, imaginatively, what others know and say and add it to their own resources. This is of course the reason why lots of verbal and social interactions with adults are so stimulating and educational for young children.

The kinds of interaction that are going to be valuable and educative for children occur in genuine partnerships where each individual's contribution is welcomed and respected. When I claim that communication and talk are the foundations of all later learning and academic achievements I do have this kind of genuine talk partnership in mind. It is no easy option and demands the time and the wholehearted involvement of parents, other carers and educators. It cannot be substituted by formal 'lessons' in talking and listening, by 'off-the-shelf' courses of the 'teach your baby to talk/read/write' kind, or by sitting children in front of the 'telly'. The latter strategy is not always a serious mistake and can be useful on occasions – television introduces children to some stunning visual aspects of the world and human knowledge. However, television is not interactive in the ordinary human communicative way and babies and toddlers will not develop full language ability by watching it. The rich potential of the electronic babysitter in the corner of the room can only be brought out by adults who share viewing with children, talk to them about it, think of things to do to follow up programmes and help their children to link television experiences to their own daily lives and activities.

Listening to children

As we nurture children's skills in communicating and talking we must also develop our own abilities as good listeners. Listening to children, including the very youngest infants, has become a matter of increasing interest to practitioners and researchers, as well as families (Clark et al. 2005). Listening to children and babies, taking their views seriously and doing something about them, are matters central to respecting children's rights, monitoring the quality of the care and education they receive and empowering them and their communities. Listening and responding to babies involves understanding that they have preferences and dislikes of a very personal kind and the sensitive carer must monitor and respond appropriately to movements, gestures, facial expressions and a considerable range of cries and vocalizations. At the heart of this is the skill of tuning in to the many different ways in which babies respond and interpreting these as communications (Mortimer et al. 2007). In order to help early years professionals tune in to babies, practitioners in Stockton-on-Tees in the UK have pioneered a method called 'Babywatch'. This begins with running observations of babies made by an experienced early years practitioner. These observations are then written up in the form of a narrative diary describing the day (or part of the day) through the eyes of the baby and in the 'voice' of the baby. The practitioners then reflect on this narrative in a structured feedback session and try to analyse critically their own behaviour and plan strategies that will make them better listeners and communicators (see Mortimer et al. 2007).

Toddlers and 3–4-year-olds in a setting can be taught to use digital cameras to make records of their 'best' or 'favourite' things, places and people. This activity can be followed up with talk about the reasons for choosing to photograph particular places and people. Other 'discussions' or child 'conferences' can be arranged to focus on relationships and the daily routines of the setting and a few open-ended questions can structure these chats with young children. Practitioners can also use observations, photos, video and sketches as evidence of children's behaviour, activities, likes and dislikes, because this too is a kind of listening to children. All these approaches were pioneered by the Mosaic approach (Clark and Moss 2001) that highlighted the 'mosaic of perspectives' needed for listening to young children. The approach emphasizes gathering many kinds of information about children's views in order to put the mosaic together for reflecting on and interpreting. The pieces of the mosaic are gathered by using practitioner observations, child conferences, cameras, 'tours' of the setting, mapping the setting and role play. The use of cameras, child-led tours of the setting, mapping favourite places and equipment and role-playing with miniature figures and equipment, all play to young children's strengths and are not reliant on the written and spoken word.

Parents, professional carers and educators

Parents and professionals must work together in partnerships of a genuine kind if their children are to thrive and be successful learners in early years settings. The case study settings in Chapters 5 and 6 have a sharp focus on partnerships between parents, educators and other carers in everything they do and have policies that are constantly evolving and being adapted by all the partners involved. This dynamic partnership approach creates the need to communicate well and keep on talking. Because of the complexities of adults' lives and the very demanding nature of working with young children in group settings, the talk is often set down as writing to be shared between all the partners. But what a wonderful example of meaningful literacy this is for the children! The written material can be anything – personal notes and letters, regular newsletters, information about the local community, invitations to social gatherings, offers of help, resources and gifts or requests for help and advice.

Most early years settings use their hall space and corridors as an information centre for sharing and exploring the curriculum with the children's families. This is mainly done by means of displays that use photos, children's work and a written account to clarify 'the why' and 'the how' of what goes on in the school. The long main corridor of Earlham Early Years Centre has become a kind of 'community conversation' recently with displays of photos from the past and the present of the nursery and many of the families can see their own family histories reflected in generations of smiling faces! Information about the current curriculum focus in each of the rooms is always displayed, along with invitations to come in and share in the children's learning. The Foundation Stage room in St John's School is itself the message and the stimulus for parents and the community to participate in and contribute to the learning.

These displays are part of a shared partnership approach, not just a semi-official information service, because parents have many opportunities to talk to all the staff about this material and suggest better ways of sharing, adapting and extending it to home life and activities with their children in their particular cultural and ethnic contexts. The sharing of information about the curriculum in Hampden Way Nursery is also done through parents' albums that are loose-leaf folders in which a particular aspect of the curriculum is explained in an accessible way. Each album is lavishly illustrated with photos of the children involved in the activity, and features examples of their work. These albums are always available to parents during the school day. Other centres use children's learning diaries to record both the children's and the practitioners' choices of special and significant achievements and samples of work. Many school classes in the Foundation Stage use a 'Home and School Diary' that goes back and forth every day to record briefly anecdotes, experiences and comments. This is a kind of ongoing conversation that keeps the channels of communication between home and school open and dynamic.

The traditional parents' evenings have also changed in most early years centres and schools and are no longer about simply giving out information, nor are they always evening events. They have become interactive workshops in which parents, carers and educators together play with the materials and resources the children use every day, listen to each other, challenge each other and explain their aspirations for the children.

Links between educators and families are very close in the Steiner Waldorf kindergartens and are often led and developed by parents who help in the schools, organize many outings and other activities, raise funds and actually make equipment for the children. In Chapter 5 mention was made of the organic vegetable garden that was developed by parents in the Cambridge kindergarten and this activity led to simple sociable lunches together after a hard morning's digging and educating. These same parents also organized expert speakers to come and visit the school and talk about gardens of many kinds.

In the Cambridge kindergarten all parents of new children are linked up with a parent who has been involved with the kindergarten for some time and are thus drawn into their partnership relationship with the school. Professional staff also go out into the community and share their expertise in child development, play and puppet-making with local playgroup leaders, and families and children using a community centre in an adjacent deprived area.

Teachers in this kindergarten regularly share with the parents their approaches to aspects of the curriculum that may not be familiar. For example, after celebrating the Hindu festival of Diwali with the children the teachers decided to send an open letter to the parents explaining why they decided to do it and how they set about making it comprehensible to the children. The letter included the Diwali story one teacher had written for the kindergarten's celebrations and details of how they involved the children at every stage, the help provided by particular parents who celebrated the festival themselves, and an account of the events of the great day.

Finally, in this school as in the London nursery, parents' evenings are 'hands-on' events in which parents are expected to do what their children do – although with far less success! Yet these playing and learning sessions for parents and early years professionals build trust and confidence and allow the talk to flow around the important topics of learning, play, literacy, mathematical thinking, the social and emotional aspects of learning in communities, and much more.

Many integrated Children's Centres have taken parental involvement much further forward and boldly entered the areas of research, psychology, child development and educational theory! Although they still invite parents to come along and do what the children do, such as messy play, small world play and gluing and sticking, they also hold sessions in which they unpack the early years jargon used by practitioners and ask parents to share their own expertise about their children with the professionals. Some settings share theories about children's thinking, as in schema theory and dispositions, and ask families to record their own observations at home and feed them into the children's records. Parents in some areas are also participating in building up their child's end of Foundation Stage Profile by contributing observations, anecdotes and photographic evidence, as well as discussing the judgements put forward by the teachers (Liverpool Framework/Liverpool City Council 2007). Perhaps one of the most heartening developments in the field of partnerships between families and early years professionals has been the involvement of fathers in many early years settings. The Liverpool project mentioned above has a Dads' Club that meets regularly and enables Dads and their young children to get together for several hours and share in the kinds of activity that they enjoy – from football to cooking, from sharing books to messing about with paint and glue or just chatting.

Partnerships between parents, professional carers and educators are about much more than sharing information on the curriculum – they are also about social and cultural life in communities and the hopes and aspirations we all have for the young children we are involved with. These projects and developments are also about the aspirations and empowerment of the parents and extended families who use early childhood settings. This makes the role of such settings of great importance because, to quote Whalley's (2007: 8) summary of the Start Right report (Ball 1994), they are:

- exemplifying good practice;
- providing information about current research;
- offering appropriate parental education and professional support;
- helping parents to develop and sustain their self-esteem and self-sufficiency.

This takes on huge significance if we bear in mind all the evidence which shows, again and again, that the key factor in the development of early literacy is not what schools do alone but what goes on at home, especially in the years before statutory schooling (pre-5 in the UK). The importance of home experiences to literacy and numeracy should keep us all talking together in early years settings for the sake of the children.

Finding our voices

We are in a period of massive changes and rapid upheavals in all aspects of early years care and education, and it is important that parents and professionals try to look further than just the needs and concerns of their own children and settings. We have to be open and flexible and ready to learn about alternative ways of approaching the early education of our youngest citizens, particularly at this time when increasingly narrow and centralized strategies are being imposed at all levels of education. The case studies in Chapters 5 and 6 are a small contribution to the processes of valuing and learning from diversity and local initiatives.

Parents and professionals have to find their voices and exercise their democratic rights and responsibilities, in order to have a say in what happens to their own young children in early years settings, in order to campaign on issues that affect all families with young children, and most importantly, in order to gain access to information about alternative views and approaches to early years care and education. One example of a different approach that made national headlines and was discussed briefly in Chapter 6 is the continental European kindergarten curriculum (Channel 4 1998). But there is also a well-established and widely researched early years curriculum promoted by educators and other professionals in the USA and the UK, which is known as the Developmentally Appropriate Curriculum (DAC) (Bredekamp 1987; Blenkin and Kelly 1996) and has the central conviction that: *'education should be shaped in accord with the learners' stage of development, and the knowledge and interests which have emanated from their experiences within the home and community'* (Hurst and Joseph 1998: 39).

This developmental curriculum does not deny the value of subjects and the many branches of human knowledge, but respects learners and the ways in which they come to understand new knowledge and information by relating them to what they know and understand already. The skills of teaching, by parents and professionals, are bound up with helping young learners make these links between new and old knowledge, observing learners closely and knowing when and how to challenge them, and supporting their self-esteem and confidence so that they are never humiliated and develop the courage to 'have a go' and even 'get it wrong'.

The approach to learning language and literacy in this book has been of this developmentally appropriate kind. For example, the emphasis on communicating and talking to babies and sharing books with them, although they may not seem to be talkers and readers, and the treating of young children's marks and scribbles as written communications, are ways of affirming that the infant is already a member of the human language and literacy club and on the way to getting better at the club's activities – with a little help and encouragement from the senior members.

If we wish to retain a developmentally appropriate curriculum for the early years there are several difficult issues that must be tackled in our shared conversations and in our contributions to national debates. Do we really want our youngest children's delight in rhymes, stories and books distorted and channelled into silly exercises with punctuation, 'sentences' and 'phonemes' (these last two features are not straightforward and are still debated by professional linguists)? Do we really feel happy about 4-year-olds regularly being taught synthetic phonics as part of a large class group, regardless of their knowledge of English, their existing literacy achievements, or their special educational, emotional and physical needs? Evidence from the USA suggests that whole class teaching of systematic phonics leaves many children indifferent, bewildered, stressed and prevented from using their emerging literacy insights (Meyer 2002). Do we find it acceptable that families are also being pressured into behaving like teachers and asked to go through strictly prescribed home reading routines 'on the assumption that literacy is about time, drill and practice' (Oldham 2008)? The intrusion of such 'drill and kill' approaches into the home environment is a matter of some concern to all who know that a love of words, stories, new information and poetry underpins the love of books and reading. An encroaching 'scholarization' of childhood and homes is the theme in one of the papers prepared for the Cambridge University Primary Review website (Mayall 2007, www.primaryreview.org.uk). Do we really believe that we can continue to build genuine partnerships between parents, educators, other professionals and local communities if parents of children as young as 4 years old are ordered to do 'homework' with them and given 'guidance' as to the duration of this in terms of minutes? What will happen to the respect and pride we should all take in those wonderful family reading lessons that happen anywhere and any time, as the following incident illustrates?

> We are waiting for a table in a 'fast food' restaurant that uses the American system of asking customers to wait to be seated, and we are standing by the large wooden notice-board that says just that. A girl of about 5 years old joins us by the notice-board and examines it intently while her mother pays at the desk for the meal they have just eaten. When her mother is ready to leave, the child pulls her towards the board and says 'Listen, mum, listen, "Please wait to be served"', pointing to the words on the notice as she reads the phrase. Mother, child and the rest of us in the queue are delighted by this demonstration, even when mum gently points out that the notice actually says, 'Please wait to be seated'. They walk off, mum saying how clever it was to get the beginning and the end of the last word right and starting to explain why the notice is about being seated rather than being served.

Grandparents are also significant as sharers of culture and literacy for many young children and they feature strongly in the research literature about language development and emerging literacy (Butler 1979; Campbell 1999; Karmiloff and Karmiloff-Smith 2001; Whitehead 2002; Jessel et al. 2004; Gregory et al. 2007). This long research history of learning with grandparents highlights the emotional charge that can transform stories and texts into meaningful cultural and social experiences for young children. Grandparents are important emotional buffers for the young and carriers of family intimacy and attachment styles across the generations (David 2006).

Looking at early years settings

Looking at early years settings – those we send our own children to, or plan to send them to, and those we work in, supervise or set up – is also part of finding our voices. Critical evaluations of our early years settings includes finding the words to describe their shortcomings and propose changes for the better. Many early years practitioners now look at their own practices and set out on a process known as action research in which they implement small changes, evaluate these carefully and move on to further improvements (Blenkin and Kelly 1997). This spiral of self-improvement works best when the children's families and local community are drawn in and become part of the process too (Whalley 2007). The particular relevance of this approach for supporting language development lies in the fact – so obvious that it is frequently overlooked – that children bring the languages, stories and communicative conventions of their homes and cultures into the settings with them. This language from home is the starting point for their future academic development, their literacy and their thinking and there can be no other starting point. It is also the bedrock of their self-esteem, cultural identity and emotional stability, so any rejection or lack of respect for it will be disastrous for the children.

A visit to a setting, or any critical evaluation of one, could well start with a look at staff attitudes to the children's home language or languages, the language policy agreed on by all the practitioners in the setting and the range and variety of language, literature and literacy experiences available to the children on a daily basis – including the littlest ones in the baby room! Guidelines for doing this can be put together from the suggestions at the end of the earlier chapters in this book and the examples of work in the case study settings in Chapters 5 and 6.

Of course we must also look at equipment and space (indoors and outside), standards of cleanliness, safety and security, the range of experiences and curriculum available and staff–children ratios and staff qualifications. But there is also the matter of 'having a vision' and this series of books is committed to a vision of early childhood learning that goes deeper than buildings, regulations and staffing. Supporting early learning emphasizes and requires respect for children as individuals, attention to equal opportunities for them to progress and develop, including equal access to good-quality early years provision, and a democratic perspective in all care and education, no matter how young and inexperienced the children in the settings (Hurst and Joseph 1998). A useful rule of thumb for assessing such important and complex features of a setting might be 'Do I feel cherished and valued here and will my child flourish here?'

Last words

This final chapter may have ranged even more widely and generally than is usual in a 'language book' but it is the privilege and the curse of language study to cross all boundaries and include just about everything. Just as we cannot separate the various aspects of language development and functions – communicating, talking, listening, reading and writing – if we are to support and nurture them effectively, so we cannot separate language from the social settings and cultures in which it is learnt and shared. Similarly, we cannot separate learning to read from love of stories and books and a deepening understanding of human behaviour, history and knowledge. Most significantly for the early years, we cannot separate learning about language and literacy from how children and families feel about their languages and themselves, or how they feel about taking on new forms and functions of language, or even a new language.

Young children have so much to learn and so much to bring to the processes of learning, but they transform everything they do with their freshness of vision and their readiness to be delighted, puzzled and challenged. They bring us their new-minted language and stop us in our stale old tracks with their observations on the new worlds they have found. We have a duty to keep their language and their vision fresh and a chance – if we are prepared to learn more about the language we think we know – to share in their explorations of language and literacy. This book is a small contribution to the learning we must be prepared to do if we are to support language development in all our children.

Summary

This final chapter returns to the power and significance of young children's drive to communicate and their developing abilities as great communicators and talkers. These abilities are linked to children's involvement in caring relationships and mutually satisfying interactions and conversations.The nature of another kind of partnership, that between parents and the professional carers and educators who work with their children, is discussed and illustrated with examples of good practice from the case study settings in Chapters 5 and 6. This discussion leads on to an analysis of the ways in which parents and professionals can use their voices to challenge inappropriate curriculum interventions and practices. The final sections of the chapter suggest ways of looking critically at early years settings and urge readers to learn more about children's language achievements.

Further reading

Abbott, L. and Langston, A. (2006) *Parents Matter: Supporting the Birth to Three Matters Framework.* Maidenhead: Open University Press.

Hurst, V. and Joseph, J. (1998) *Supporting Early Learning: The Way Forward.* Buckingham: Open University Press.

Makin, L. and Whitehead, M. (2004) *How to Develop Children's Early Literacy: A Guide for Carers and Educators.* London: Paul Chapman.

Nutbrown, C., Hannon, P. and Morgan, A. (2005) *Early Literacy Work with Families: Policy, Practice and Research.* London: Sage Publications.

Whalley, M. (2007) *Involving Parents in their Children's Learning*, 2nd edn. London: Paul Chapman.

Appendix I

The Bears' Treasure Island

Chapter 1

One grey Tuesday two bears (that were born in Switzerland) were walking in Norwich, they saw a castle. They used a rope to climb in it. They saw a pig. The pig said, 'My name is Babe. What's yours?' 'My name is Berny, his is Switzerland,' said one bear. They all climbed back down. But before they get to the end of the rope it snaps. Berny and Babe fall on land. Berny twists his leg. Switzerland falls on a rock. He jumps on the next rock and jumps on land. Switzerland saves them from being shot. Babe and Switzerland carry Berny home.

Chapter 2

They all made friends with Babe, and Babe meets Ted (the leader), Electro and Ivy. Ted shows Babe his bear print machine. Ivy gets his tennis set. He finds a map on his ball. He pulls the elastic band off. Ted tells Ivy to pull the lever and get Electro. Electro tells them, 'It is a treasure map.'

Chapter 3

They get on the ship and set off, they sail for three days. Suddenly they see twenty pirate ships. 'Throw two anchors!' Shouts Ivy. One anchor falls in the sea, the other sinks a pirate ship. Ivy and Berny and Switzerland and Babe board the ship. Babe snorts in the Captain's eyes. The Captain says, 'Men, get him!!' A pirate throws a sword through

Babe's collar. Babe went flying. The sword sticks in a sail. The pirates throw three darts at Babe. They miss. Berny sees Babe. Berny falls in a cannon. The cannon is lit and Berny goes flying. He falls in the sea. Switzerland and Ivy jump to Babe and Berny. They save them. They jump on their ship. They tell Electro and Ted what happened.

Chapter 4

Ted looked through a telescope and saw an island that glistened in the light. Ted tells them it is Treasure Island. They saw ten pirate ships near the island. They shoot down nine ships. They get to the island. They sail straight at the ship. It cracks in half and the pirates drown.

Chapter 5

They all get off the ship. And dig where the map says. Berny and Switzerland went down into the hole. When they said that they had found the treasure, Babe held one end of the rope and gave the other end to the bears down the hole. They tied it to the treasure chest and Babe pulled them up. They find a piece of paper that says,

TO FIND THE KEY, GO TO SEA, YOU MUST SEE,
A BIG 'T', THEN YOU WILL HAVE THE KEY.

They go to the ship. Ted reads it and says, 'We will look tomorrow.' Then they all went to bed.

Chapter 6

In the middle of the night when everyone on the ship was sleeping (except Berny and Switzerland), pirates crept on the ship. They stole the treasure. Berny and Switzerland got up, Berny tried to wake up the others, Switzerland went to stop the pirates. The others woke up. The pirates ran away.

Chapter 7

In the morning Babe, Ivy, Berny and Switzerland get off the ship. Switzerland slips on the mud into the mud. He gets out, rolls on the grass and leaves. He scares the pirates into quicksands with giant pythons and scorpions around. Switzerland washes in the sea. Berny rushes in the air and grabs the treasure. 'Bye, bye suckers!' he says to the drowning pirates.

Chapter 8

They get on the ship and sail back. The next day they get to Waterfall Island. Ivy, Switzerland, Berny and Babe get on the island. (Ivy puts some string in his jumper). Berny stops, Switzerland starts slipping down a waterfall. Berny shouts, 'Waterfall, waterfall, waterfall!!' Switzerland fell down. Babe walks in front of Berny. Berny holds on to his collar and Babe goes zooming through the water. Babe trips back on to land. Berny goes flying through the chimney of his house. Ivy uses his string to save Switzerland. He lands on Ivy. Switzerland gets up and sees the key and shouts, 'We have got the KEY!' Babe looks up and sees a rock shaped like a 'T'. When they get back to the ship they tell Ted and Electro the whole story.

Chapter 9

While the others were sailing home, Berny got a party ready. He hung up balloons around Ted's bear print machine and put honey buns, honey cake, fruit and pig food on the table. When he had finished he put a note on the door. And went to get the water.

TO TED, ELECTRO, BABE AND SWITZERLAND,
COME IN THE BEAR PRINT MACHINE.

When the others came back they looked at the note and went to the machine.

Chapter 10

They got outside, Berny said, 'We can have a party for the rest of the day!' First they played 'Pin the Tail on the Teddy' and 'Musical Teddies', 'Pig Parcel', 'Piggy in the Middle', 'Find the Pig' and other games. Then they played with the balloons. Ted moved around the machine and made bear prints. After the party they wrote a book called 'The Bears of Treasure Island' and every bear had a copy of it. They all stayed together and had adventures happily ever after.

The Teddy Team

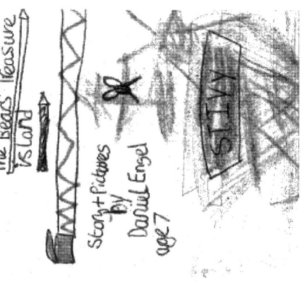

Figure AI.1 The cover of the children's book.

• • • Appendix II

Hampden Way Nursery School documents

Activity Planning Sheet

Week beginning...........

Adult:	Area of Learning:
Learning Intentions:	
Activity:	Equipment:
Language:	
Learning Outcomes:	
Next Steps:	
Evaluation:	

Garden Planning   Week beginning..........

Board learning Intentions	AOL

	Physical (including climbing and wheeled toys)	Water	Sand	K&U	Imaginative Role Play/ Small World	Construction
M						
T						
W						
T						
F						

	Movement area	Music	ICT	Maths	Art Workshop	CL&L	Dig Pits
M							
T							
W							
T							
F							

	Mon	Tues	Weds	Thurs	Fri
Evaluation AM					
Evaluation PM					

Appendix III

'The Five Year Old Steiner Waldorf Child' statement

The Five Year Old Steiner Waldorf Child

The curriculum which we follow provides a sound base for the development of formal skills and indeed many of our kindergarten activities are precursors to numeracy and literacy. However, our educational approach is premised on a developmental view of the child which recognises an optimum time for teaching the three Rs. This 'readiness' to learn – to be formally instructed – correlates with the process of maturation which usually occurs during the seventh year. Our principal approach to not forcing early literacy and numeracy means that children from Steiner Waldorf Kindergartens often enter state education without having had formal training in these areas. Naturally our kindergarten teachers and parents are concerned that bright, enthusiastic children who enter school without this training, run the risk of being labelled as 'special needs' children. We would ask you to bear this in mind when considering a child from one of our kindergartens.

Our own curriculum aims and objectives for the young child are as follows:

- To recognise and support each stage of child development
- To provide opportunities for children to be active in meaningful imitation
- To provide an integrated learning experience
- To enable child initiated creative play
- To encourage social and moral development

- To provide a safe child-friendly environment
- To work with rhythm
- To work with parents.

A Steiner Waldorf kindergarten child will have experienced a rich variety of learning situations, all of which are related to the daily business of living. They will have had opportunities for the development of mathematics and linguistics but through integrated rather than subject-based activities. (Maths for example, might have taken place around the cooking table.) We feel that learning gains meaning and relevance by being embedded in a social context. Children will have learnt many songs, poems and stories 'by heart not head'. We place great emphasis on the oral tradition of *telling* rather than reading stories and many of our children have good aural skills, excellent memories and extended vocabularies. Our five year olds will have gained a degree of manual dexterity through activities such as sewing, weaving, drawing and painting. They will also have had plenty of opportunity for social and imaginative play which aids concentration and develops social skills. They will have learnt to care for their environment and for each other and will have experienced the importance of daily, weekly and yearly rhythms. Festivals, which deepen and enrich the experience of childhood, will have played an important part in their time at kindergarten.

Earlham Early Years Centre documents

Communication, Language and Literacy Policy

Aim

To support and develop the skills children need to formulate and express their needs, thoughts and feelings. To encourage them to use communicative strategies to assert their individual identity, build self-esteem, initiate and enhance relationships, make sense of the world and get things done.

Context

Areas of learning in the Foundation Stage curriculum.
Links to the learning culture section of the Centre's Ethos Policy.

How do we do this?

By acknowledging and respecting the language and communication strategies that children bring from home.

- Encouraging the children to express themselves confidently, using a range of strategies and resources.
- Encouraging good eye contact.
- Modelling good listening, non-verbal strategies, being a writer, being a reader and using language in a rich variety of ways.
- Modelling talk and questioning skills through meaningful conversation and discussion with children.
- Introducing appropriate vocabulary.

- Planning opportunities for non-verbal communication, talking, listening, emergent reading and emergent writing.
- Planning activities that strengthen and support physical control, coordination and expression.
- Providing a range of fiction and non-fiction materials and spaces to explore them.
- Providing books, tapes and videos to borrow.
- Planning a range of opportunities for adults and children to share books.
- Introducing a rich variety of stories, languages, rhymes, songs, music and sounds to explore.
- Providing a print-rich learning environment to stimulate children's awareness of print.
- Providing a variety of resources for mark-making.
- Using role play, small-world play, puppets and storytelling to provide opportunities for the children to develop their own narratives and to use as a stimulus for listening, talking, reading and writing.
- Providing an environment that encourages spontaneous singing and dancing.

The adult role in supporting the five dispositions in the curriculum

Common themes in the adult role across the five dispositions:

- the ability of the adult to recognize and give status to what is important to the child;
- commentating;
- involvement as the professional;
- modelling;
- emotional support, respect, warmth and laughter;
- creating a safe setting in which the children can learn and grow (trust between professionals);
- acting as a bridge between the centre and the community;
- professional courage (swimming against the stream);
- planning and extending;
- orchestrating imaginative activities for children to explore;
- protecting children's time.

Bibliography

Aardema, V. and Vidal, B. (1981) *Bringing the Rain to Kapiti Plain*. London: Macmillan.

Abbott, L. and Langston, M. (2006) *Parents Matter: Supporting the Birth to Three Matters Framework*. Maidenhead: Open University Press.

Ahlberg, J. and Ahlberg, A. (1977) *Each Peach Pear Plum*. Harmondsworth: Kestrel Books/Penguin.

Ahlberg, J. and Ahlberg, A. (1981) *Peepo*. Harmondsworth: Kestrel Books/Penguin.

Aitchison, J. (1989) *The Articulate Mammal: An Introduction to Psycholinguistics*. London: Routledge.

Aitchison, J. (1997) *The Language Web* (1996 BBC Reith Lectures). Cambridge: Cambridge University Press.

Almon, J. (1997) The importance of play as a foundation for creative thinking. Keynote address at the University of Plymouth Conference, 'Realizing Children's Potential: The Value of Early Learning', 6 September, Plymouth.

Altwerger, B. (ed.) (2005) *Reading for Profit: How the Bottom Line Leaves Kids Behind*. Portsmouth, NH: Heinemann.

Alwyn, J. (1997) Lifting a veil on language in the kindergarten, in *Early Childhood: A Steiner Education Monograph*. Forest Row: Steiner Education UK.

Angelou, M. (1984) *I Know Why the Caged Bird Sings*. London: Virago.

Ball, C. (1994) *Start Right: The Importance of Early Learning*. London: RSA.

Barrett, G. (1986) *Starting School: An Evaluation of the Experience*. Norwich: AMMA.

Beard, R. (1995) *Rhyme, Reading and Writing*. London: Hodder & Stoughton.

Bennett, N. and Kell, J. (1989) *A Good Start? Four Year Olds in Infant Schools*. Oxford: Blackwell.

Bettelheim, B. (1976) *The Uses of Enchantment: The Meaning and Importance of Fairy Tales*. London: Thames & Hudson.

Bissex, G.L. (1980) *GNYS AT WRK: A Child Learns to Write and Read*. Cambridge, MA: Harvard University Press.

Bissex, G.L. (1984) The child as teacher, in H. Goelman, A. Oberg and F. Smith (eds) *Awakening to Literacy*. London: Heinemann.

Blakemore, S.J. and Frith, U. (2005) *The Learning Brain: Lessons for Education*. Oxford: Blackwell.

Blenkin, G.M. and Kelly, A.V. (eds) (1996) *Early Childhood Education*, 2nd edn. London: Paul Chapman Publishing.

Blenkin, G.M. and Kelly, A.V. (eds) (1997) *Principles into Practice in Early Childhood Education*. London: Paul Chapman.

Bredekamp, S. (1987) *Developmentally Appropriate Practice in Early Childhood Programs Serving Children from Birth through Age 8*. Washington, DC: National Association for the Education of Young Children.

Bredekamp, S. and Rosegrant, T. (eds) (1992) *Reaching Potentials: Appropriate Curriculum and Assessment for Young Children*, vol. 1. Washington, DC: National Association for the Education of Young Children.

Brooker, E. (2002) *Starting School: Young Children Learning Cultures*. Buckingham: Open University Press.

Browne, A. (1981) *Hansel and Gretel*. London: Julia Macrae.

Browne, A. (2007) *Teaching and Learning Communication, Language and Literacy*. London: Paul Chapman Publishing.

Browne, E. (1994) *Handa's Surprise*. London: Walker Books.

Bruce, T. (ed.) (2006) *Early Childhood: A Guide for Students*. London: Sage Publications.

Bruce, T. and Spratt, J. (2008) *Essentials of Literacy from 0–7*. London: Sage Publications.

Bruner, J.S. (1976) Nature and uses of immaturity, in J.S. Bruner, A. Jolly and K. Sylva (eds) *Play: Its Role in Development and Evolution*. Harmondsworth: Penguin.

Bruner, J.S. (1983) *Child's Talk: Learning to Use Language*. Oxford: Oxford University Press.

Bruner, J.S. (1996) A little city miracle, in Reggio Emilia *The Hundred Languages of Children*. Reggio Emilia: Reggio Children.

Bryant, P.E. and Bradley, L. (1985) *Children's Reading Problems*. Oxford: Blackwell.

Butler, D. (1979) *Cushla and Her Books*. Sevenoaks: Hodder & Stoughton.

Campbell, R. (1999) *Literacy from Home to School: Reading with Alice*. Stoke-on-Trent: Trentham Books.

Carle, E. (1970) *The Very Hungry Caterpillar*. London: Hamish Hamilton.

Carr, M. (2001) *Assessment in Early Childhood Settings: Learning Stories*. London: Paul Chapman Publishing.

Carr, M. and May, H. (2000) 'Te Whariki: curriculum voices', in H. Penn (ed.) *Early Childhood Services: Theory, Policy and Practice*. Buckingham: Open University Press.

Carroll, L. ([1865] 1998) *Alice's Adventures in Wonderland* and *Through the Looking-Glass*. Harmondsworth: Penguin.

Channel, 4 (1998) 'Too much too soon', *Dispatches*, 29 January.

Chomsky, N. (1957) *Syntactic Structures*. The Hague: Mouton.

Chukovsky, K. (1963) *From Two to Five*. Berkeley, CA: University of California.

Clark, A., Kjarholt, A.T. and Moss, P. (2005) *Beyond Listening: Children's Perspectives on Early Childhood Services*. Bristol: Policy Press.

Clark, A. and Moss, P. (2001) *Listening to Young Children: The Mosaic Approach*. London: National Children's Bureau.

Clark, M.M. and Waller, T. (eds) (2007) *Early Childhood Education and Care: Policy and Practice*. London: Sage Publications.

Claxton, G. (1997) *Hare Brain, Tortoise Mind*. London: Fourth Estate.

Cooper, H. (1993) *The Bear Under the Stairs*. London: Doubleday/Picture Corgi.

Cooper, H. (1995) *Little Monster Did It!* London: Doubleday/Picture Corgi.

Cooper, H. (1996) *The Baby who Wouldn't go to Bed*. London: Doubleday/Picture Corgi.

David, T. (2006) Grandparents matter, in L. Abbott and A. Langston (eds) *Parents Matter*. Maidenhead: Open University Press.

Deacon, A. (2002) *Slow Loris*. London: Hutchinson.

DCSF (Department for Children, Schools and Families) (2007) *The Children's Plan: Building Brighter Futures*. Norwich: The Stationery Office.

DCSF (Department for Children, Schools and Families) (2008a) 'Confident, capable and creative: supporting boys' achievements' Guidance for practitioners in the Early Years Foundation Stage (www.standards.dcsf.gov.uk).

DCSF (2008b) *Fairplay: A Consultation on the Play Strategy*. London: DCSF.

DfEE (Department for Education and Employment) (1998) *The National Literacy Strategy: Framework for Teaching*. London: DfEE.

DfES (Department for Education and Skills) (2002) *Birth to Three Matters: A Framework to Support Children in their Earliest Years*. London: DfES.

DfES (Department for Education and Skills) (2006) *Independent Review of the Teaching of Reading. Final Report*. Nottingham: DfES.

DfES (Department for Education and Skills) (2007a) *The Early Years Foundation Stage*. London: DfES.

DfES (Department for Education and Skills) (2007b) *Letters and Sounds: Principles and Practice of High Quality Phonics*. London: DfES.

Department for Education and Skills (DfES) Sure Start Unit (2002) *Birth to Three Matters: A Framework to Support Children in their Earliest Years*. London: DfES.

Dombey, H. (2006) How should we teach children to read? *Books for Keeps*, 156: 6–7.

Edgington, M. (2004) *The Foundation Stage Teacher in Action: Teaching 3, 4 and 5-year-olds*, 3rd edn. London: Paul Chapman Publishing.

Engel, D.M. and Whitehead, M.R. (1993) More first words: a comparative study of bilingual siblings. *Early Years*, 14(1): 27–35.

Engel, S. (1995) *The Stories Children Tell: Making Sense of the Narratives of Childhood*. New York: W.H. Freeman.

EYCG (Early Years Curriculum Group) (1992) *First Things First: Educating Young Children: A Guide for Parents and Governors*. Oldham: Madeleine Lindley.

Featherstone, S. (2006) *'L' is for Sheep: Getting Ready for Phonics*. Lutterworth: Featherstone Education Ltd.

Felix, M. (1975) *The Little Mouse Trapped in a Book*. London: Methuen.

Fox, C. (1993) *At the Very Edge of the Forest: The Influence of Literature on Storytelling by Children*. London: Cassell.

Gamble, N. and Yates, S. (2007) *Exploring Children's Literature: Teaching the Language and Reading of Fiction*, 2nd edn. London: Paul Chapman.

Gardner, H. (1991) *The Unschooled Mind: How Children Think and How Schools Should Teach*. London: Fontana.

Gentry, J.R. (1982) An analysis of developmental spelling in GNYS AT WRK, *The Reading Teacher*, November: 192–200.

Gerhardt, S. (2004) *Why Love Matters: How Affection Shapes a Baby's Brain*. Hove: Routledge.

Goldschmied, E. and Jackson, S. (2004) *People Under Three*, 2nd edn. London: Routledge.

Goleman, D. (1995) *Emotional Intelligence: Why It Can Matter More Than IQ*. London: Bloomsbury.

Goncu, A. and Gaskins, S. (eds) (2006) *Play and Development: Evolutionary, Sociocultural and Functional Perspectives*. NJ: Lawrence Erlbaum Associates.

Gorman, T. and Brooks, G. (1996) *Assessing Young Children's Writing: A Step by Step Guide*. London: Basic Skills Agency/NFER.

Goswami, U. (2008) *Cognitive Development: The Learning Brain*. Hove: Psychology Press.

Goswami, U. and Bryant, P.E. (1990) *Phonological Skills and Learning to Read*. Hove, UK: Lawrence Erlbaum Associates Ltd.

Graham, A. and Gynell, D. (1984) *Arthur*. Harmondsworth: Penguin.

Gregory, E. (2008) *Learning to Read in a New Language*, 2nd edn. London: Sage Publications.

Gregory, E., Arju, A., Jessel, J., Kenner, C. and Ruby, M. (2007) Snow White in different guises: interlingual and intercultural exchanges between grandparents and young children at home in East London, *Journal of Early Childhood Literacy*, 7(1): 5–25.

Gregory, R.L. (1977) Psychology: towards a science of fiction, in M. Meek, A. Warlow and G. Barton (eds) *The Cool Web*. London: Bodley Head.

Hall, N. (1987) *The Emergence of Literacy*. Sevenoaks: Hodder & Stoughton.

Hall, N. and Martello, J. (eds) (1996) *Listening to Children Think: Exploring Talk in the Early Years*. London: Hodder & Stoughton.

Hall, N. and Robinson, A. (2003) *Exploring Writing and Play in the Early Years*, 2nd edn. London: David Fulton.

Halliday, M.A.K. (1975) *Learning How To Mean: Explorations in the Development of Language*. London: Arnold.

Hardy, B. (1977) Towards a poetics of fiction: an approach through narrative, in M. Meek, A. Warlow and G. Barton (eds) *The Cool Web*. London: Bodley Head.

Harris, M. (1992) *Language Experience and Early Language Development: From Input to Uptake*. Hove, UK: Lawrence Erlbaum Associates Ltd.

Hasan, R. (1989) The structure of text, in M.A.K. Halliday and R. Hasan (eds)

Language, Context and Text: Aspects of Language in a Social-semiotic Perspective. Oxford: Oxford University Press.

Hayes, S. and Ormerod, J. (1988) *Eat Up, Gemma*. London: Walker Books.

Heath, S.B. (1983) *Ways with Words: Language, Life and Work in Communities and Classrooms.* Cambridge: Cambridge University Press.

Heath, S.B. (1997) New directions in youth development: implications for schooling? Paper presented at the Institute of Education, University of London Conference, 'Literacy: From Research to Practice', 13 December, London.

Holland, P. (2003) *We Don't Play With Guns Here: War, Weapon and Superhero Play in the Early Years.* Maidenhead: Open University Press.

Hoodless, P. (1996) Children talking about the past, in N. Hall and J. Martello (eds) *Listening to Children Think: Exploring Talk in the Early Years.* London: Hodder & Stoughton.

Hurst, V. and Joseph, J. (1998) *Supporting Early Learning: The Way Forward.* Buckingham: Open University Press.

Hutchins, P. (1968) *Rosie's Walk.* London: Bodley Head.

Hutchins, P. (1981) *Alfie Gets In First.* London: Bodley Head.

Iannucci, A. (1998) Stir crazy, *Guardian*, 31 March.

Jeffers, S. and Chief Seattle (1991) *Brother Eagle, Sister Sky.* Harmondsworth: Penguin.

Jenkinson, S. (1997a) As ye sow so shall ye reap, *Steiner Waldorf Kindergarten Newsletter*, Autumn/Winter.

Jenkinson, S. (1997b) Voices on the green: the importance of play, in *Early Childhood: A Steiner Education Monograph.* Forest Row: Steiner Education UK.

Jenkinson, S. (1997c) The genius of play. Paper presented at the University of Plymouth Conference, 'Realizing Children's Potential: The Value of Early Learning', 6 September, Plymouth.

Jenkinson, S. (2001) *The Genius of Play.* Stroud: Hawthorn Press.

Jessel, J., Gregory, E., Islam, T., Kenner, C. and Ruby, M. (2004) Children and their grandparents at home: a mutually supportive context for learning and linguistic development, *English Quarterly*, 36(4): 16–23.

Jones, R. (1996) *Emerging Patterns of Literacy: A Multidisciplinary Perspective.* London: Routledge.

Kalliala, M. (2006) *Play Culture in a Changing World.* Maidenhead: Open University Press.

Karmiloff, K. and Karmiloff-Smith, A. (2001) *Pathways to Language: From Fetus to Adolescent.* Cambridge, MA and London: Harvard University Press.

Katz, L. (1995) *Talks with Teachers of Young Children.* Norwood NJ: Ablex.

Kent, G. (1997) Information technology: exploiting the learning potential with early years children, *Early Childhood Review: Papers from GAEC*, 4: 4–8.

Kress, G. (1997) *Before Writing: Rethinking the Paths to Literacy.* London: Routledge.

Kress, G. (2000) *Early Spelling: Between Convention and Creativity.* London: Routledge.

Lewis, D. (2001) *Reading Contemporary Picturebooks: Picturing Text.* London: Routledge.

Liverpool Framework/Liverpool City Council (2007) *Let's Work Together: A Liverpool Framework for Supporting Children's Learning by Working in Partnership with Parents*. Liverpool: Liverpool City Council.

Lofdahl, A. (2005) 'The Funeral': a study of children's shared meaning-making and its developmental significance, *Early Years*, 25(1): 5–16.

McArthur, T. (1995) Rhythm, rhyme and reason: the power of patterned sound, in R. Beard (ed.) *Rhyme, Reading and Writing*. London: Hodder & Stoughton.

McKee, D. (1980) *Not Now, Bernard*. London: Andersen.

Makin, L. and Whitehead, M. (2004) *How to Develop Children's Early Literacy: A guide for Carers and Educators*. London: Sage Publications.

Manning-Morton, J. and Thorp, M. (2003) *Key Times for Play: The First Three Years*. Maidenhead: Open University Press.

Matthews, J. (2003) *Drawing and Painting: Children and Visual Representation*, 2nd edn. London: Paul Chapman Publishing.

Medlicott, M. (1997) Storytelling: the essential art of speaking and listening. Paper presented at the Institute of Education, University of London Workshop Seminar, 'Developing language in the Early Years', 23 June, London.

Meyer, R.J. (2002) *Phonics Exposed: Understanding and Resisting Systematic, Direct, Intense, Phonics Instruction*. NJ and London: Lawrence Erlbaum Associates, Inc.

Miller, L. (1996) *Towards Reading*. Buckingham: Open University Press.

Moore, R.S. and Moore, D.N. (1975) *Better Late Than Early: A New Approach for Your Child's Education*. New York: Reader's Digest Press.

Morris, D. (1991) *Babywatching*. London: Jonathan Cape.

Mortimer, H./Stockton Borough Council (2007) *Listening to Children in their Early Years*. Stafford: QEd Publications.

Moyles, J. (ed.) (2007) *Early Years Foundations: Meeting the Challenge*. Maidenhead: Open University Press.

Murray, L. and Andrews, L. (2000) *The Social Baby: Understanding Babies' Communication from Birth*. Richmond: The Children's Project.

Nabuco, E. and Sylva, K. (1996) The effects of three early childhood curricula on children's progress at primary school in Portugal. Paper presented at the ISSBD Conference, Quebec, 12–16 August.

Nelson, K. (1989) *Narratives from the Crib*. Cambridge, MA: Harvard University Press.

Newkirk, T. (1984) Archimedes' Dream, *Language Arts*, 61(4): 341–50.

Nicol, J. (2007) *Bringing the Steiner Waldorf Approach to your Early Years Practice*. Abingdon: Routledge.

Nutbrown, C. (1998) Early assessment: examining the baselines, *Early Years*, 19(1): 50–61.

Nutbrown, C., Hannon, P. and Morgan, A. (2000) *Early Literacy Work with Families: Policy, Practice and Research*. London: Sage Publications.

Oldham, J. (2008) Don't take it as read: a disturbing bedtime story, *Books for Keeps*, 169: 3–4.

Paley, V.G. (1981) *Wally's Stories: Conversations in the Kindergarten*. Cambridge, MA: Harvard University Press.

Paley, V.G. (1986) *Mollie is Three: Growing Up in School*. Chicago: University of Chicago Press.

Payton, S. (1984) Developing awareness of print: a young child's first steps towards literacy, *Education Review Offset Publication No. 2*, Birmingham: University of Birmingham.

Pinker, S. (1994) *The Language Instinct: The New Science of Language and Mind*. Harmondsworth: Allen Lane/Penguin.

Potter, B. ([1908] 1989) The Tale of Jemima Puddle-Duck, in *The Complete Tales of Beatrix Potter*. London: F.W. Warne.

Qualifications and Curriculum Authority/Department for Education and Employment (QCA/DfEE) (2000) *Curriculum Guidence for the Foundation Stage*. London: QCA.

Rawson, M. (ed.) (1997) *Steiner Waldorf Education: Aims, Methods and Curriculum*. Forest Row: Steiner Education UK.

Reddy, V. (1991) Playing with others' expectations: teasing and mucking about in the first year, in A. Whiten (ed.) *Natural Theories of Mind*. Oxford: Blackwell.

Reggio Emilia (1996) *The Hundred Languages of Children: A Narrative of the Possible*. (catalogue of the exhibit). Reggio Emilia: Reggio Children.

Riley, J. (2006) *Language and Literacy 3–7: Creative Approaches to Teaching*. London: Paul Chapman.

Rousseau, J.J. ([1762] 1991) *Emile*. London: Dent.

Saxe, R. and Baron-Cohen, S. (eds) (2007) *Theory of Mind*: A Special Issue of *Social Neuroscience*. Hove: Psychology Press.

Schaffer, H.R. (ed.) (1977) *Studies in Mother–Infant Interaction*. London: Academic Press.

Schweinhart, L. and Weikart, D. (1997) *Lasting Differences: The High/Scope Pre-school Curriculum Comparison Study Through Age* 23. Ypsilanti, MI: High Scope Press.

Scrivens, G. (1995) Where's the 'K' in emergent literacy: nursery children as readers and writers, *Early Years*, 16(1): 14–19.

Sendak, M. (1967) *Where the Wild Things Are*. London: Bodley Head.

Serpell, R., Baker, L. and Sonnenschein, S. (2005) *Becoming Literate in the City: The Baltimore Early Childhood Project*. Cambridge: Cambridge University Press.

Sherman, A. (1996) *Rules, Routines and Regimentation: Young Children Reporting on their Schooling*. Nottingham: Educational Heretics Press.

Siraj-Blatchford, I., Sylva, K., Mattock, S., Gilden, R. and Bell, D. (2002) *Researching Effective Pedagogy in the Early Years*. (REPEY) DfES Research Report 356. London: HMSO.

Smith, B.H. (1981) Narrative versions, narrative theories, in W.J.T. Mitchell (ed.) *On Narrative*. Chicago: University of Chicago Press.

Smith, F. (1988) *Joining the Literacy Club*. London: Heinemann.

Stannard, J. and Huxford, L. (2007) *The Literacy Game: The Story of the National Literacy Strategy*. Abingdon: Routledge.

Steptoe, J. (1987) *Mufaro's Beautiful Daughters*. London: Hamish Hamilton.

Stern, D. (1977) *The First Relationship: Infant and Mother*. London: Fontana.

Sylva, K., Melhuish, E., Sammons, P., Siraj-Blatchford, I. and Taggart, B. (2004) *The Effective Provision of Pre-School Education (EPPE) Project. Technical Paper 12. Final Report*. London: DfES/Institute of Education, University of London.

Thornton, L. and Brunton, P. (2007) *Bringing the Reggio Approach to your Early Years Practice*. Abingdon: Routledge.

Tizard, B. and Hughes, M. (2002) *Young Children Learning*, 2nd edn. Oxford: Blackwell.

Torrey, J.W. (1973) Illiteracy in the ghetto, in F. Smith (ed.) *Psycholinguistics and Reading*. New York: Holt, Rinehart and Winston.

Tovey, H. (2007) *Playing Outdoors: Spaces and Places, Risk and Challenge*. Maidenhead: Open University Press.

Trevarthen, C. (1993) Playing into reality: conversations with the infant communicator, *Winnicott Studies*, 7: 67–84.

Trevarthen, C. (2002) Learning in companionship, *Education in the North: The Journal of Scottish Education*, 10: 16–25.

Vipont, E. and Briggs, R. (1969) *The Elephant and the Bad Baby*. London: Hamish Hamilton.

Vygotsky, L.S. (1978) *Mind in Society: The Development of Higher Psychological Processes*. Cambridge, MA: Harvard University Press.

Waddell, M. (1990) *Rosie's Babies*. London: Walker.

Wade, B. and Moore, M. (1993) *Bookstart in Birmingham*. London: Book Trust.

Wade, B. and Moore, M. (1996) Children's early book behaviour, *Educational Review*, 48(3): 283–8.

Wade, B. and Moore, M. (1997) Parents and children sharing books: an observational study, *Signal*, 84: 203–14.

Wagner, J. and Brooks, R. (1977) *John Brown, Rose and the Midnight Cat*. Harmondsworth: Penguin.

Weddell, C. and Copeland, J. (1997) The bad news: TV your children really watch, *The Australian*, 18 September.

Weinberger, J. (1996) *Literacy Goes To School: The Parents' Role in Young Children's Literacy Learning*. London: Paul Chapman Publishing.

Weir, R.H. (1962) *Language in the Crib*. The Hague: Mouton.

Wells, G. (1987) *The Meaning Makers: Children Learning Language and Using Language to Learn*. Sevenoaks: Hodder & Stoughton.

Whalley, M. (2007) *Involving Parents in their Children's Learning*, 2nd edn. London: Paul Chapman Publishing.

White, D. (1954) *Books Before Five*. New Zealand: NZ Council for Educational Research.

Whitehead, M.R. (1990) First words: the language diary of a bilingual child's early speech, *Early Years*, 10(2): 53–7.

Whitehead, M.R. (2002) Dylan's routes to literacy: the first three years with picture books, *Journal of Early Childhood Literacy*, 2(3): 269–89.

Whitehead, M.R. (2004) *Language and Literacy in the Early Years*, 3rd edn. London: Paul Chapman.

Whitehead, M.R. (2007) *Developing Language and Literacy with Young Children*, 3rd edn. London: Paul Chapman Publishing.

Whybrow, I. and Reynolds, A. (1999) *Harry and the Bucketful of Dinosaurs.* London: David and Charles.

Winnicott, D.W. (1971) *Playing and Reality.* Harmondsworth: Penguin.

Zipes, J. (1979) *Breaking the Magic Spell: Radical Theories of Folk and Fairy Tales.* London: Heinemann.

Useful websites

www.booksforkeeps.co.uk – Books for Keeps
www.booktrusted.com – the Book Trust
www.clpe.co.uk – the Centre for Literacy in Primary Education
www.childrenslaureate.org – the Children's Laureate
www.deni.gov.uk – Northern Ireland Department for Education
www.ecm.gov.uk – Every Child Matters
www.learning.wales.gov.uk – Welsh Department for Education and
    Training
www.ncb.org.uk – the National Children's Bureau
www.outdoorclassrooms.co.uk – Outdoor Classrooms
www.primaryreview.org.uk – The Primary Review, University of
    Cambridge
www.scotland.gov.uk – Learning and Teaching Scotland
www.signsforsuccess.co.uk – teaching signing
www.standards.dcsf.gov.uk/primaryframeworks – Department for
    Children, Schools and Families, England
www.steinerwaldorf.org.uk – Steiner Waldorf UK
www.talktoyourbaby.org.uk – the early language campaign of the National
    Literacy Trust

Index